DR. SHARALYN MARIE PAYNE

UNSTUCK.
UNLEASHED.
UNSTOPPABLE.

INSPIRATION, MOTIVATION, *and* STRATEGIES *to* HELP YOU MOVE OUT *of* NEUTRAL *and* SUPERCHARGE YOUR SUCCESS

UNSTUCK. UNLEASHED. UNSTOPPABLE.
Inspiration, Motivation, And Strategies To Help You Move Out Of
Neutral And Supercharge Your Success
© 2017 by Dr. Sharalyn M. Payne

All rights reserved. No part of this book may be reproduced or utilized in any form or by any means, electronic or mechanical, photocopying, recording or by any information storage and retrieval system, without permission in writing from the publisher. Address all inquiries to:

Push Partner
2450 Lakeside Parkway
Suite 150-1018
Flower Mound, TX 75022
United States of America
Telephone: 707-654-9464

Print ISBN: 978-1-945464-20-1

eBook ISBN: 978-1-945464-21-8

Cover design by: Purple Magnolia

Interior design by: Lisa Thomson

Scripture quotations marked NLT are taken from the Holy Bible, New Living Translation, copyright ©1996, 2004, 2007. Used by permission of Tyndale House Publishers, Inc., Carol Stream, Illinois 60188. All Rights Reserved.

Dedication

To all who have and will determine that a life of wealth, power, and freedom is the only way to live;

To those who annihilate the enemy every chance they get;

To all those who have ever felt like giving up but found the courage and strength to hold on another day;

To those who truly believe they are destined to live an extraordinary life; and finally,

To the love of my life, my mother, Ella G. Payne.

UNSTUCK. UNLEASHED. UNSTOPPABLE.

UNSTUCK. UNLEASHED. UNSTOPPABLE.

Acknowledgments

I owe a special thanks to so many people who hold a special place in my heart. I thank each of you for helping to make this labor of love possible. So many people have helped to mold me into the person I am today and have been instrumental in the creation of this project. I would love to offer special thanks to the following people:

- How do you say thank you to the person whose life means everything to you? How do you say thank you to the person who is your silent heartbeat? How do you say thank you to the one who you would move heaven and earth for, if you had the power? How do you say thank you to your favorite girl? How do you say thank you to your cheerleader and your best friend? Mama, I don't know how to say thank you in such a way that you could truly feel my love, appreciation, and admiration for you. While the words may fail to express my love for you, I pray that I live my life in such a way that says, "Thank you." Thank you for being my mother, my advisor, my director, my coach, my encourager, my friend, my confidante, and my supporter. Thank you for being you.

- Daddy, thank you for giving me a determination to overcome obstacles. The gift you gave me is not one that I would have chosen for myself, but it is one that has made everything else possible. So, thank you.

- Thank you to my little sister, Shondra, for your belief in me. Thank you for pushing me. Thank you for encouraging me. Thank you for beautiful words spoken in some of my hardest places. I will never forget my favorite quote—words spoken by you in my darkest, loneliest, hardest hour.

- Thank you to my brother-in-love for your care and concern.

- Thank you to my "favorite aunts" for being examples of godly women along with my mother and my godmother. Aunt Sherion,

Genie, and Phreida—thank you for being there. Thank you for being more than aunts; thank you for being my friends and my support system. Thank you, Aunt Sherion, for showing me what love, friendship, support, family, faithfulness, and kindness looks like wrapped in beauty. Thank you, Aunt Genie, for showing me bravery, courage, and responsibility. Thank you, Aunt Phreida, for your sound advice and for always having a listening ear. Aunt Lisa—thank you for making me laugh and for remembering to laugh no matter what life may bring. Aunt Rosie—thank you for your encouraging words.

- To my godmother, Miss Mary, I am so grateful my mother chose you to be my godmother. Thank you for all of your prayers and encouragement.

- Leebo—I finally did it. You have been pushing me to write a book for years. Thank you for seeing what I didn't.

- Thank you to my team for providing invaluable support. Latoya, you have been a true Godsend. Kim, Hanne, Lynn, and Lyndsay for your patience and your creative genius.

- I sincerely want to thank everyone who attempted to block, hinder, or impede my success because you positioned me to fly like an eagle, fight like a champion, battle like a warrior, and rise like the Phoenix. Without you, this book would not be possible.

Most of all, I would like to thank God for rescuing me and saving me from myself. Thank you, God, for being the Master Weaver and for orchestrating EVERYTHING in my life to work for my benefit. Thank you for every gift, every strength, and every talent that enables me to fulfill my purpose on this earth. Thank you for trusting me with your people. Thank you for wrapping me in your arms. Thank you for amazing me. It is my heart's deepest desire that I am a woman after your own heart. One day, I will feel your heartbeat. Thank you for loving me in spite of...

Contents

Introduction 1

It's Important That You Not Allow Everyone to Speak into Your Life 3

Your Life Depends on Your Ability to Avoid Danger—No Matter
How Appealing It May Appear 5

Positivity Attracts and Negativity Retracts 9

Empires Are Built On the Backs of Critics 11

I Don't Want Anyone Who Doesn't Want Me 13

Are you a Talker or a Doer? 15

Want to Get More Out of Life? 17

Are You Allowing a Setback to Deter You from Achieving Your Goals? 19

Do You Have Dreams or Do You Have Goals…and Do You
Know the Difference? 21

Action Always Beats Intention 23

Trust and Forgiveness Are Not One and the Same. 25

What Type of Leader Are You? 27

Do You See People as They Are or as You Want Them to Be? 29

Are You a Willing Contributor to Someone Else's Success? 31

Accomplish What Appears to Be the Impossible Dream 33

In Spite of What Others May Say, Your Past Does Not
Define You; Unless You Let It 35

You Teach People How to Treat You 37

What Goals Are You Willing to Die Having Left Undone? 39

What Story Have You Created in Your Mind that is Not True
and is Keeping You from Accomplishing Your Goals? 41

How to Recover from Disappointment 43

Be Very Careful How You Handle Me 46

No Matter Who You Are and What You Do, Not Everyone Will Like You 49

Do You Know Someone Who Is More Focused on Criticizing Others
Than They Are with Improving Themselves? 52

Are You Dying Without Having Lived? 55

Five Simple Steps to Overcome Negative Thinking 57

Are You One of the Most Beautiful People in the World? Find Out Now 60

How Do You Deal with Life Challenges? 63

What Is the Reason People Come into Our Lives? 65

Does Money Change Who You Are? 67

How Do You View the Negative Experiences of Life? 69

What is Holding You Back from Getting the Love You Deserve? 71

How to Effectively Handle Your Haters 73

Strategies for Responding to Adversity 76

What Happens When You Decide to Achieve the Big Dream for Your Life? . . . 79

How Do the People in Your Life Make You Better? 81

The #1 Key to Getting What You Want and It Has
Nothing to Do with Action. 83

The #1 Self Destructive Behavior That Can Ruin Your Life 86

How Does Your Partner Treat You?. 88

What Would Happen if You Devoted More Energy to
Achieving Your Dreams? 90

Do You Wear Out the Tough Situation, Or Does It Wear Out You?. 92

Do You Have True Friends and More Importantly:
Are You a True or Fair-Weather Friend? 94

How Long Are You Willing to Pay for Someone Else's Offenses? 97

Are You for Sale? 99

What Would You Accomplish if Your Talent Was Backed by Hard Work? . . . 101

Are You Letting a Lack of Vision and Creativity
Hold You Back from Living the Life of Your Dreams?. 103

How Strong is Your Foundation When It Has Been Shaken? 105

Do Your Friends Deserve You and Do You Deserve Your Friends?. 108

Go, Be Great 111

Why Is Time More Precious than Money? 113

How Do You Show the People You Love That They Are Loved? 115

How Badly Do You Want to Be Successful? 117

What Does Your Name Say About You? 119

What Have Your Failures Taught You? 121

Are You a Sure Thing? 123

Do You Underestimate Your Value in Relationships? 125

How Does Controversy and Challenge Define You? 128

Are You Living Your Goals or Someone Else's? 130

How Big Are Your Goals? 132

Have You Ever Suffered So Greatly That All You Could Do Was Pray? 134

What Has Been the Hardest Lesson You Have Had to Learn? 136

What Are You Waiting on to Begin to Live a Life of Purpose? 138

Are You Fierce and Fearless? 140

Have You Ever Thought Your Critics May Be Onto Something? 143

Are You Sacrificing Your Spirit for the Approval of Others? 146

Have You Ever Been Way in Over Your Head…Or Am I Alone? 149

Are You the Same Person Post-Adversity That You Are Pre-Adversity? 151

How Do You Climb the Mountain When You've Been in the Valley? 154

What Are the Benefits of Knowing You? 157

Do You Let Challenges Stop You from Achieving Your Goals? 159

Do You Use Your Words to Create and Shape the Life You Want? 162

How Competitive Are You? 164

Are You Governed by How You Feel? 166

What's Your Grit Factor? 168

What Excuses Are You Making Because You Failed to Execute Properly? ... 170

Are You Aware of the Number of People Who Are Watching You? 172

Do You Often Feel Misunderstood When Sharing Your Dreams? 174

Do You Allow the Actions of Others to Extinguish Your Flame? 176

Do You Fight Back and Win? 178

Have You Ever Made a Decision That You Later Regretted? 181

Whose Opinion is More Valued? Your Own or the Naysayers? 184

Do You Have What It Takes to Win Against Someone
Just as Stronger, if Not Stronger, Than Yourself? 186

How Resourceful Are You? 188

Bitter or Better? 190

How Committed Are You to the Things that Really Matter to You? 192

Do You Learn from Your Defeats? 194

What's the Difference Between Temporary Defeat and Failure? 196

What Does Pressure Do to You and for You? 198

What Do You Want More Than Success? 200

Do Your Actions Support Your Words? 202

What Goal Are You Ready to Give Up On, but the Reason Why You
Want to Accomplish It Makes You Hold On Just a Little While Longer? 204

Are You Living Life on Your Own Terms? 206

When Was the Last Time You Thanked Your Haters? 208

How Do You Best Solve Problems? How Has That Been Working for You? ... 210

How Do You Make the Best Use of Your Time? 212

How Are You Really Doing?. 214

Are You the Active Architect of Your Life?. 216

Can You See Your Dreams Even When You're Sleeping? 218

Are You More Like the Scarecrow or the Lion? 220

Do You Know Who You Are and Whose You Are? 222

Your Heart Is Deceptive. 224

How Often Do We Question That What We See and Hear
Is Accurately Being Depicted?. 226

What Are You Willing to Sacrifice for Your Dreams? 229

When You Finish Speaking, What Do People Think of You? 231

How Do You Appreciate in Value Because Others Are
Appreciative of What You Mean to Them? 234

Have You Ever Received What You Prayed for to Later Regret it? 237

You Can Run, But You Cannot Hide 239

Tools and Resources for Extraordinary Success. 241

Book Dr. Sharalyn to mobilize, inspire, and empower your group!. 242

Marked. Success on Purpose. 243

Push Partner University. 244

Bring *Unstuck, Unleashed, and Unstoppable*
to Your Home or Enterprise 245

About the Author 246

UNSTUCK. UNLEASHED. UNSTOPPABLE.

Introduction

Ask God for the world because He just might give it to you.
– Shondra Van Buren

I was at home speaking to my little sister—who hates when I call her my little sister—about how I was just worn out with everything that was happening in my life at the time. While I wasn't overwhelmed, I was definitely stressed. I had been under pressure for so long that I had a short fuse and in a moment of frustration, I was really short and crisp with her. A moment that I wasn't proud of at all. I apologized to her and while speaking with her about what was happening in my world, she simply said these words which amazed me and spoke to me in such a way that I will never forget. I have taken the words she spoke in my hour of need and etched them deep, deep, in my heart, and my hope for you is that you will do the same.

We all have had experiences in life that could have made us broken, bitter, or better. We all have had dreams for our life that we wanted so badly to accomplish. We all have wanted to make something out of the life that we have been given. It is up to us to push forward and to make the most out of every opportunity. It is up to us to escape the prison we are in and live a lifestyle of freedom. It is up to us to be seekers of truth and wisdom, and apply these principles to experience a joy, a peace, and a happiness that can only happen if we embrace every moment.

It is in this spirit that I hope you will go on a journey of success and decide that you will no longer be stuck, but you will be free. I hope on your life's journey you will choose to not allow life to shake you, but that you will remain unshakeable. I hope you will be inspired, equipped, and encouraged by the lessons I've learned to become unstuck and unstoppable while unleashing your greatness. And when you do, I hope you will ask God for the world because He just may give it to you.

UNSTUCK. UNLEASHED. UNSTOPPABLE.

UNSTUCK. UNLEASHED. UNSTOPPABLE.

It's Important That You Not Allow Everyone to Speak into Your Life

Put up some walls.
– Joel Osteen

Don't take in what everyone says to you. Consider both the message and the source. Don't give everyone permission to speak into your life. Sometimes the words people speak can be powerful, catapulting you to the next level. The words can be awe-inspiring and motivational. Other times, the words can cause you to question yourself and the decisions you have made for your life. The words can have a negative effect and send you into a downward spiral. I remember when an associate told me what her friends had been saying about me. I had to shut the conversation down immediately. I knew that she and her friends were not people who I respected or admired, so why would I consider their opinions of me? It wasn't that I thought they were beneath me; I just didn't feel that they had a vested interest in my success.

I knew they were a little intimidated by my position in their circle. I entered their world with a previous history with their leader and a connection that went back years. In their minds, the favor and relationship that I had with their leader posed a threat to their position.

You cannot always take in what someone is saying and allow it to impact who you are.

They didn't understand that I am a loner by nature. Although I had history with the leader, we were not as close as they perceived. So, when they attacked my character, I knew who I was and I knew that what they were saying wasn't true.

I sincerely believed the comments were coming from their own insecurities, and they were attempting to project those insecurities on me. I was able to not take in what they were saying and allow it to affect me, but also to distance myself from those types of people. I was able to remain cordial, while not allowing their opinions to impact me and damage myself or the relationships they were attacking. Imagine how I felt when I received a phone call a few months later apologizing for the comments and questioning whether we could build a friendship.

Along the same lines, I met someone I tremendously respected. During a disagreement, there were some negative comments that were said, which contradicted all of the positive comments the person had just made regarding me the day before. Which comments was I to believe—the positive words spoken when everything was good, or the negative words spoken in anger? Were you flattering me before to get what you wanted, or were you speaking truth in anger because the scheme didn't work? How do you really feel about me? The point I want to get across is that you cannot always take in what someone is saying and allow it to impact who you are.

What has someone said that you need to shake off? What can you do or say when people begin to speak negatively in your life without your permission?

UNSTUCK. UNLEASHED. UNSTOPPABLE.

Your Life Depends on Your Ability to Avoid Danger— No Matter How Appealing It May Appear

Never wound a snake, kill it.
– Harriet Tubman

A snake is a snake is a snake. A snake will always be a snake and a snake is synonymous with deception. As a single woman, I have a tremendous amount of respect for men who are honest with me up front and give me a choice of whether I want to willingly participate in the world they are offering. No one wants to be deceived. I remember being introduced to a gentleman and asking him if he was involved with someone else. He led me to believe that he wasn't seeing anyone. We never entered into a relationship, but we did go out from time to time over the course of three years, as well as spend a lot of time with his family, including holidays. I knew that if I allowed myself to completely let go, I could become absolutely crazy in love with him. Things were easy when we were together. We had an undeniable chemistry and we often talked about what it would be like for us to have a future together.

> As a single woman, I have a tremendous amount of respect for men who are honest with me up front and give me a choice of whether I want to willingly participate in the world they are offering.

UNSTUCK. UNLEASHED. UNSTOPPABLE.

On a Friday night in May, we went to dinner and had a great time together as usual. After dinner, he looked into my eyes and told me that he wanted me to know that he would never intentionally hurt me. He said it again and asked me if I believed it and if I understood what he was saying. At that moment, he never expounded on the comment and for whatever reason, I didn't ask him. Over the weekend, I would play that comment over and over again. By Monday, I realized that he was saying something without saying it. So, I called him and asked him about it. He told me that he didn't want to discuss it over the phone, but would tell me in person the next time we went out. I was frustrated. I hung up the phone and knew I needed to put my thoughts in writing.

I thought I was writing a note in my phone or sending myself a text about the conversation. What I didn't know was I had somehow mistakenly sent him a text message saying if he really cared about me, he would just come clean and be honest with me. He immediately called me and told me that he was getting married to his ex-girlfriend. Supposedly, they had been broken up for about three years, but they had remained friends. He would go on to tell me that he loved me as well, but that he had dated her for about five years before they broke up, and she would be devastated if he married someone else. As a man, he could be happy either way—with me or with her. The difference maker for him was that he believed me to be stronger and in a better place financially. Eventually, he would tell me she was pregnant.

He would continue to call me and ask me to hang out or go out to dinner. He felt like we needed to stay in touch and remain friends. In my mind, we were not friends because everything was based upon him displaying snake-like characteristics. He deceived me. Whenever we would discuss if he was either in a relationship or seeing someone else, he told me he wasn't. Had he told me differently, I would have never involved myself with him in any capacity. There were many dialogues of me telling him how I was disappointed that he would call and tell me he wanted to pursue something more serious between us when he knew his heart was elsewhere and that he was still involved with this woman. He would tell me that the decision to marry involved several other factors and not just love, because he loved me, not taking anything away from her. He would say that you never knew what the future held, and if they weren't together for any reason, he would marry me the next day. I knew that there was no way we would ever be together, because I would not be able to accept that he willingly deceived me. If I continued to talk to him and be friends with him, I would possibly be holding out hope that we would be together one day, because we both agreed that our being together seemed very natural and organic. However, the truth was our foundation as friends was built on deception. We never had a chance. So, I couldn't remain friends. If he would lie to me continuously about no one else in the picture, hide that he was dating and subsequently, engaged, marry based upon a lie, and attempt to convince me to continue with things the way they were prior to him getting married, I have to acknowledge that he was a beautiful snake. If I chose to pet the snake by continuing to deal with him, I couldn't become upset if the venom killed me. It was necessary for me to kill the snake and walk away. I am so happy that I had enough love and respect for myself to set some boundaries and destroy the thing that could have destroyed me.

 What do you need to walk away from?

UNSTUCK. UNLEASHED. UNSTOPPABLE.

Positivity Attracts and Negativity Retracts

Every positive thought propels you in the right direction.
– Unknown

Life has thrown me some blows from which I thought I would never recover. There have been some battles that left me almost hopeless. What helped me make it through my dark nights and lonely hours was saturating myself with positive thoughts, affirmations, and positive people. I found that when I focused on the "what if this happens" scenarios, I usually felt defeated. I began to see that in actuality, I was preparing for a negative outcome. Subconsciously, I was training my mind to focus on what I didn't want, which was a negative situation instead of what I did want, which was for things to be the way I desired and pictured. If we focus on positive thoughts, we open ourselves up to infinite possibilities that could blow our minds and produce our desired outcome. We then begin to vibrate at a different level and that vibration draws positive energy to come our way. I'm not saying it is always easy to be positive because it's not. What I truly believe is that positive thoughts move us closer to our goals and negative thoughts move us further away from our goals. So, think of it like this: You are on the ladder of success which has thirteen steps. Right now, you are standing on rung seven. There are six steps beneath you representing the wrong direction, and six steps above you representing the right direction. For every positive thought, you ascend the ladder one rung at a time, moving toward your goals and dreams. As you think negatively, you descend the ladder, moving away from your dreams and goals. If you could visualize this image every time you had a negative thought, would you begin to immediately replace your negative thoughts with positive thoughts, thereby transforming your life's story?

 Where are you on the ladder of success? What negative thoughts do you need to replace with positive thoughts?

UNSTUCK. UNLEASHED. UNSTOPPABLE.

Empires Are Built On the Backs of Critics

*Critics are like the supporting actors in your movie.
Their role is ultra-important to your success, for their energy propels you to stardom.*
– Sharalyn Payne

Are you ever fueled by the energy that is created when you know people are looking at you and waiting for you to fail? I have been all too familiar with this energy. Although it is uncomfortable, it provides me with the fuel I need to give it all I've got—to leave everything on the line. It's kind of like their hatred and desire to see me fail creates an unbelievable determination to succeed. It's like I suddenly become Superwoman and Batwoman at the same time. I feel like I am Rocky. I can hear the music playing repeatedly in my mind. It's like I can see flashes of Muhammad Ali press conferences and fights.

> *I wonder if my haters and secret enemies know that they give me way too much power. Their blatant dislike and disdain generates something inside of me that makes me feel invincible.*

I wonder if my haters and secret enemies know that they give me way too much power. Their blatant dislike and disdain generates something inside of me that makes me feel invincible. I use their negative energy to give me the fire needed to focus on success and to not let go, until I accomplish my goal. Their desire to see me fail gives me faith like a bulldog and determination like a pit bull. When my enemies eyes are on me, I couldn't fail if I wanted to…because I am trusting my gut more, I am designing a plan, and executing a strategy. My haters and enemies breed the competitive spirit I have within myself to bet on me and to ensure I am successful.

I remember I had a manager who hated my guts and would always try to set me up for failure. It was hilarious to watch the things she would try to do. None of her tricks worked, because while she was focused on her emotions, I was focused on my strategy. I was focused on executing every task with excellence and precision in spite of all her antics, instead of using my finite energy to expose her for who she really was.

> *My haters and enemies breed the competitive spirit I have within myself to bet on me and to ensure I am successful.*

While she was trying to show me up, she wasn't noticing that I was gaining a reputation of being strong, strategic, professional, and smart. Simultaneously, she was damaging her own reputation. In the end, I received a promotion with a substantial financial increase and she didn't last much longer at the organization. Her negative energy was what I needed to push me further along on my success journey.

Let your critics ignite a fire deep within your soul to achieve extraordinary success with every fiber of your being. And while doing so you'll see that they can serve as the catalyst you need to make your biggest dreams come true. Use the energy of haters, skeptics, cynics, doubters, and critics to help you gain momentum and maximize your potential.

How have you benefitted from the ill treatment of others? Who wants you to fail? How can you use that energy to push you to become better?

UNSTUCK. UNLEASHED. UNSTOPPABLE.

I Don't Want Anyone Who Doesn't Want Me

Never make a man tell you twice that he doesn't want you.
– Judge Lynn Toler

I remember being so crazy about one gentleman in particular, and I was convinced that I wanted to spend the rest of my life with him. We often discussed marriage and our future. There came a time when he began to say that I deserved better than him, and my response was always that I didn't want better, I wanted him. Boy, was I blinded by what I thought was love! Thank God I am so much wiser now!

Today, if a man told me that, I would take off running. I would probably even leave my shoes. As the song says, everybody plays the fool. What a fool I was at the time! I did deserve better than what he was offering. He was successful, handsome, charismatic, and giving. Yet, there were some other traits he had as well—characteristics and behaviors that weren't good for me. Years into the relationship, I would find out just what he meant when he would say I deserved better. What I learned would rock and shatter my world! The aftereffects of dealing with such a large personality were unbelievable. This was my story in learning the lesson that when a man tells me that he doesn't want me, I should thank him and run like hell, because the next time may not be so nice. If I had simply accepted what he said the first time, I would

> *When a man tells me that he doesn't want me, I should thank him and run like hell, because the next time may not be so nice. If I had simply accepted what he said the first time, I would have saved myself hurt, pain, time, money, shame, and humiliation.*

have saved myself hurt, pain, time, money, shame, and humiliation. Lesson learned, and this is one mistake I won't let happen again.

 Who is telling you that they don't want you (job, mate, or friend), and why are you are still holding on? What is it about you that wants someone that doesn't want you?

UNSTUCK. UNLEASHED. UNSTOPPABLE.

Are you a Talker or a Doer?

The way to get started is to quit talking and begin doing.
– Walt Disney

Have you ever met someone who is always talking about what they are going to do but never takes action? When you hear those people, what thoughts come to mind? I would have to say it depends on the person. Some people say they are going to do something and before you know it, it's done…finished. There are others that talk about what they are going to do and while you may never say it, you know they are just talking. Nothing will ever come from what they say because they are "all talk."

I decided quite some time ago to stop talking about what I was going to do or what I was working on, but to just create a plan, take action, and get started. I am naturally attracted to energy and motion. Don't get me wrong, I like hearing people talk about their dreams and goals, but I am ignited, inspired, and invigorated when I see people taking action to make it happen! For me, talking is irrelevant and unacceptable. I have got to get up and just get it done! Once I begin doing the work to make my dream a reality, I no longer like to talk about it unless I am speaking about it with someone who can actually help me (encouragement, direction, support, etc.).

There is research out there to indicate we are more likely to accomplish our goals by not talking about them. I remember growing up hearing a wise man say, "Talk is cheap; it takes money to buy land." I don't want to waste another minute talking when I could be much more productive by doing. What really helped me was making the decision to give my words life by changing my words from nouns to verbs. Now I don't talk about what I am going to do. My conversation now is focused on what I accomplished and how I did it. I no longer get the up-front satisfaction and admiration of people who are anticipating the end goal or the hateful remarks from jealous or negative associates.

UNSTUCK. UNLEASHED. UNSTOPPABLE.

Now I receive the intrinsic satisfaction of knowing I am working on a goal that is so big to me that I cannot talk about it at this moment, which I have found to be much more rewarding. Since I adopted this new approach, I am 40 percent more productive and have less stress in knowing that all eyes are no longer watching to see if my goal becomes a reality.

Tip: Instead of saying I am going to _____, try saying I have been _____. You fill in the blank.

What do you need to stop talking about doing and just start doing?

UNSTUCK. UNLEASHED. UNSTOPPABLE.

Want to Get More Out of Life?

The more you are in a state of gratitude, the more you will attract things to be grateful for.
– Unknown

Life owes us nothing, so it's best to be appreciative because things could be so much worse. One of my mother's pet peeves, which has been passed on to me, is an attitude of gratitude. It drives us up the wall to do something for someone who doesn't take three seconds to simply say thank you. *Thank you* are two words which say so much about how you feel and who you are. Gratitude makes us appreciative of what has been done and when you show appreciation, you position yourself for more.

When I showed my mother I was thankful for the first car, it positioned me to get the second car. When someone has shown me they are thankful for what I have done for them, I think they understand that I didn't have to do anything. The appreciation actually makes me want to do more for them. So, the next time they need my assistance I am more willing to help. When someone doesn't say "thank you" or show appreciation (no matter how much or little I helped), I actually wonder if they really needed or valued my help at all. The next time they need something, I have to more closely consider and evaluate if it is the best use of my time or resources because I could always help someone else who would be most appreciative.

> *Life owes us nothing, so it's best to be appreciative because things could be so much worse.*

I have found that by always looking for something to be grateful for, I always have something for which I can be grateful and appreciative.

UNSTUCK. UNLEASHED. UNSTOPPABLE.

It's as if God is rewarding me for not taking His grace, mercy, and gifts for granted. The rewards He has bestowed on me have been numerous—prosperity, health, peace, joy, laughter, movement, as well as an escape from calamity, danger, and sickness. Every moment there is something to be thankful for. I don't express my gratitude to get more things; instead I do so like a skilled farmer. As I sow gratitude, I reap more blessings to be thankful for. It is a cycle that I am not deserving of, that I cannot pay for, but I am extremely grateful to have in my life.

> When someone doesn't say "thank you" or show appreciation (no matter how much or little I helped), I actually wonder if they really needed or valued my help at all. The next time they need something, I have to more closely consider and evaluate if it is the best use of my time or resources because I could always help someone else who would be most appreciative.

What are you grateful for? I am grateful that I can breathe on my own. I have food, shelter, clothing, good health, and I am in my "right state of mind," in spite of all the pain I have been through. I have the activity of my limbs, gainful employment, spared from some of the things that others have had to encounter such as sickness. I am grateful for my family and loved ones. I am grateful that God's hand is on my life. I am grateful for every opportunity. As I have gotten older, I have even learned to become grateful for life's tough blows because without those, I probably wouldn't have grit and tenacity. We all have so much to be thankful for and about.

 What are you grateful for? Start looking for opportunities to express gratitude. Begin a gratitude journal.

Are You Allowing a Setback to Deter You from Achieving Your Goals?

Giving up on your goal because of one setback is like slashing your other three tires because you got a flat.
– Christine Kane

No one in their right mind would slash three tires because one tire has a flat. So, why would you allow one setback to deter you from accomplishing your goal? What if the setback was strategically designed to determine how badly you really wanted the goal?

I remember going to grad school, which was two and a half hours away from the city in which I lived. Classes were held during the week and at that time I was working full time. I knew someone who wanted to go to the same graduate school as well. We decided that we could carpool to alleviate the burden of having to drive two and a half hours, one way, twice per week, while working a full-time job. Just as soon as we put the plan in place, she made the decision to relocate. What was I to do? I hated to drive and I did not want to drive that many hours by myself. I could have given up on my goal of going to grad school altogether or even transferred to another school, but I was determined to go to that particular university because it was a better fit for me. I made up my mind to continue on with the plan and not let the change of plans deter me from the bigger goal.

UNSTUCK. UNLEASHED. UNSTOPPABLE.

I drove alone the first day of class and the drive wasn't as bad of a drive as I originally thought, although I certainly didn't want to do it a couple of times a week by myself. Once I got to class, I met another group of ladies with the same goal. We exchanged numbers and decided to carpool together. This time, instead of two chicks taking turns driving, there would be four of us. What a relief! Although I never had the same set of ladies to carpool with, I always had a set of goal-oriented women to carpool with during my tenure at that university, which aided in making my goal of obtaining my graduate degree achievable. Even better, we had so much fun and I was able to build a network of pretty sharp people. The graduate degree was beneficial in opening many doors for me throughout my career. What if I had allowed the initial setback to prevent me from achieving my goals?

 What goals do you need to go back and revisit? I once heard someone say that a setback is nothing but an opportunity for a comeback. Start working on your comeback, because it's time.

Do You Have Dreams or Do You Have Goals…and Do You Know the Difference?

A dream becomes a goal when action is taken toward its achievement.
– Bo Bennett

Many of us inaccurately label our dreams as goals instead of calling the dream what it really is: just a wish, if we are not working on making it a reality. Let me be clear. There is nothing wrong with having a dream. Dr. Martin Luther King, Jr. had a dream, but he made his dream a catalyst for a goal by working to actualize his dream. Dr. King did not just wish for something to happen. He wasn't content with the idea that his dream would one day become true. He took aggressive action to make the dream that we talk about today a reality. Because he understood that for us to enjoy the liberties in his dream, effort would be required for achievement. The same holds true for each one of us that has a dream. No matter how big the dream or how small the dream, it is not a goal unless we take action to accomplish what is deep in our hearts.

> *Many of us inaccurately label our dreams as goals instead of calling the dream what it really is: just a wish, if we are not working on making it a reality.*

One of my dreams was becoming an author. I would never have accomplished this goal until I took action towards making it a reality. I placed it in front of me so that I could see it every day. Subconsciously, my mind began to work on the goal of me becoming an author. Topics

> *No matter how big the dream or how small the dream, it is not a goal unless we take action to accomplish what is deep in our hearts.*

would come to me throughout the day for me to write about. I began to use my phone to capture the topics so I wouldn't forget them. Other ideas worthy to write about began to come to me as well. I began to journal and keep a note pad nearby. One day, I decided to tune out all the noise and just sit down and write. I could have analyzed it and thought about it and talked about it, but the goal of becoming an author required me to sit down and discipline myself to make it happen. It required me to give up some other pleasurable activities in order to find time to write, if I really wanted to become an author. My dream required me determining in my mind that another year would not pass by without written material out in the universe for someone to read. The dream of becoming an author required the action of acting like an author (writing) on a consistent basis until I had something out there. I am a goal- and action-oriented individual who turns my dreams into reality. I refuse to die only a dreamer. Dreams are just the beginning. Take the next step. Get moving.

What dream do you need to turn into goal? What action is needed to make your dream a reality?

UNSTUCK. UNLEASHED. UNSTOPPABLE.

Action Always Beats Intention

The smallest deed is better than the greatest intention.
– John Burroughs

Stop right now and ask yourself what goal do you need to stop intending to do and start doing. Why is the word "intend" normally followed by an excuse or a reason, as some people like to say? I intended to go back to school, but…I intended to go visit, but…

Those who accomplish greatness resist the urge to give into intention and its evil cousin excuses. Achievements demand action. Actions will always surpass intentions. Intentions are an enemy of success and stand in between you and your goal. No more, no less. One thing I have always been known for is my ability to execute. It drives me absolutely crazy to hear people talk about what they intend to do. I always think don't intend to do, just do. Life happens and things will always come up. You must determine that you will accomplish whatever you intend to do, whatever it is that you set your mind to achieve. There is no stopping you if you decide to take action, even if it is a small step. Consistent action yields progress and trumps intention every single day of the week. Become a person of action and not one of intentions and willful thoughts. Become disciplined enough to get back on track if you somehow find yourself off course because life got in the way. Decide you will substitute the words ***I did*** for *I intended*.

UNSTUCK. UNLEASHED. UNSTOPPABLE.

I remember going through a pretty rough period in life. I was laid off, among other things. For about a week, I just could not shake the fact that I was back in the job market. I was frustrated and agitated that all the minorities were impacted. I could not believe that in the twenty-first century, with our first African-American president, we were still dealing with such overt racism. I determined that I could not and would not allow this situation to go unnoticed. Because I am committed to making a positive impact on humanity, I took action to remedy the situation and make things better for those coming after me. It was as if I could not rest until I did something. During that time period, there were other things that I needed to work on simultaneously. When I looked up a few weeks later, I found there were some things that I wanted to do (intended to do), but I hadn't done. I was so disappointed in myself. I buckled down, drafted a plan, and began to take massive action to bridge the gap between what I intended to do and what should have been accomplished by that time period to get back on track. Although I was working on a worthy cause, I still had no excuse for not achieving the other goals I had set.

> *You must determine that you will accomplish whatever you intend to do, whatever it is that you set your mind to achieve.*

> *Decide you will substitute the words **I did** for I intended.*

What did you intend to do that you need to go back and just do? Remove the obstacles and get it done. Remember, people are attracted to people of action and execution, not those of intention. Who are you?

UNSTUCK. UNLEASHED. UNSTOPPABLE.

Trust and Forgiveness Are Not One and the Same

Forgiveness we are commanded to do, but trust must be earned.
– Bishop T. D. Jakes

Forgiveness can be so hard. Sometimes, we find that those closest to us betray and hurt us. There have been times in my life when I have felt that those near and dear to my heart crushed my spirit. I remember once thinking I was so in love with someone who proved not to be worthy of the love I had to offer. I spent years listening to him apologize time after time and asking for my forgiveness. As a lover of God and a believer of His word, I have no choice but to forgive.

If I, with all of my imperfections, desire forgiveness, then I must be willing to forgive those who have wronged me, no matter what was done.

If I, with all of my imperfections, desire forgiveness, then I must be willing to forgive those who have wronged me, no matter what was done. I'm not saying I have been able to forgive overnight or even the next week. What I am saying is that when I have found that the hurt was too deep for me to get over, I prayed extensively that God would give me a heart of forgiveness.

What I am saying is that when I have found that the hurt was too deep for me to get over, I prayed extensively that God would give me a heart of forgiveness.

There have been times when I forgave someone for how they treated or handled me, but due to the severity of the action, I could not automatically restore the relationship. It was important for me to exercise wisdom. Wisdom required me to assess the situation and determine if myself and the offender should: engage in dialogue about the occurrence and move forward together, discontinue the relationship altogether, or continue the relationship and work on rebuilding the trust, which was broken.

Going back to the earlier situation with the person who I thought at the time I was in love with but who had betrayed me…I had to forgive him, but I did not have to continue on with the relationship. To continue on with the relationship without demanding that he earn my trust was, in essence, saying that I condoned and accepted the inappropriate behavior. If he truly loved me and wanted my forgiveness and reconciliation, then he would have been willing to do the hard work of earning my trust. Needless to say, he was committed to asking for forgiveness but uncommitted to re-earning my trust. It takes time to build trust but only moments to destroy it. Forgiveness and trust are not one and the same. Both require action.

Who do you need to ask for forgiveness and do the hard work of rebuilding trust? Who do you need to forgive, but require they respect and value the relationship enough to put the work into rebuilding trust so the foundation for the future can be unshakable?

UNSTUCK. UNLEASHED. UNSTOPPABLE.

What Type of Leader Are You?

Leaders must be tough enough to fight, tender enough to cry, human enough to make mistakes, humble enough to admit them, strong enough to absorb the pain, and resilient enough to bounce back and keep on moving.
– Jesse Jackson

> *Leaders don't allow unfortunate situations to stifle or hinder their progress, but they have grit and keep moving when others would allow pain and failure to paralyze them.*

So often, we look at leaders as if they are invincible, as if they are not human, as if they cannot be touched. Leadership is influence and there is a leader in all of us. We all have someone that we can influence. Leaders in positions of authority and in the spotlight are human. They bleed red blood and have emotions just like each of us. Leaders worth following are in touch with their feelings. They can be moved with the cares of this world. When faced with injustice, they stand up and fight for worthy causes. When wrong, leaders admit their mistakes. When unsure and after they have vetted an idea, leaders take risks and go with their gut. In the face of failure, leaders re-assess and look at the situation for feedback and as an opportunity to learn. Leaders don't allow unfortunate situations to stifle or hinder their progress, but they have grit and keep moving when others would allow pain and failure to paralyze them. Leaders resist the urge to give up on dreams worth achieving and never stay down.

Whenever I reflect on this quote, I think of the late Bishop G.E. Patterson, a leader who marched with Dr. King for civil rights, cried when he was voted Presiding Bishop because he knew what the weight of the office and what the position entailed, and forgave and restored those who had betrayed him. The late Bishop Patterson was strong enough to confront the defiant, humble enough to admit both his pain and his mistakes, and resilient enough to keep moving ahead and making plans for the next generation, even when faced with a death sentence from cancer. In my humble opinion, that's a leader who is worth noticing, worth following, worth studying, and worth taking copious notes on.

Look back at your own life. When have you demonstrated these leadership characteristics? Now ask yourself, "Am I a leader that others can admire?" Why or why not? What do you need to change?

UNSTUCK. UNLEASHED. UNSTOPPABLE.

Do You See People as They Are or as You Want Them to Be?

When people show you who they are, believe them the first time.
– Dr. Maya Angelou

Years ago, I met a co-worker and we became relatively close. Approximately five years into our friendship, there came a time in our relationship when she showed me she was not the person I thought she was. We collaborated on a few projects and made plans for some pretty important things to happen, but at the ninth hour, she backed out. She began to play games and dodge phone calls. Her actions placed me in a pretty tight situation. Nonetheless, I viewed the situation as her not wanting to tell me that she had a change of heart. After a couple of weeks went by, we discussed the incident and she gave me her viewpoint. I felt she wasn't being entirely forthcoming because she had that information prior to her suggesting we engage in the project. I valued the friendship, and we picked back up and eventually got back to a good place.

Years later, I was offered a great opportunity, but I needed several references. I asked her if she would be willing to provide a favorable reference for me and she agreed. In my mind, I thought she would be perfect because she knew both my character and my capabilities. We had worked together before, and I had just completed a couple of projects pro bono in my area of expertise a few weeks prior. Imagine my surprise when I received a phone call that they were unable to make contact with her to conduct the reference check. I was in disbelief. I asked for an opportunity to contact her and have her to connect with the person doing the check. They gave me the approval to do so with a time constraint. I reached out and called the person who I thought was my friend. We spoke of the urgency of the situation, and I asked her to please reach out the following day to the organization's representative who was responsible for background checks. Although she agreed, she didn't keep her word. Again, I received a call from the representative indicating that they tried reaching out to her, but to no avail. When I spoke with my former co-worker, she admitted to me that they had been calling her, but she simply didn't have the time to talk to them and she wasn't in a good mood. Her refusal to participate in my success nearly cost me the opportunity. Luckily, I had a mentor that I told the story to and he made a suggestion. The suggestion ended up working out for me. Because she failed to answer a few questions regarding me, I had to jump through so many hoops it was unbelievable. I often think that she showed me who she was years prior, but I chose not to accept what she showed me about her true character because I wanted to believe differently about her. My lack of seeing her for who she was almost cost me something valuable.

> *I often think that she showed me who she was years prior, but I chose not to accept what she showed me about her true character because I wanted to believe differently about her. My lack of seeing her for who she was almost cost me something valuable.*

Who has shown you they should not be in the current position they are in your life, and you are hoping for something different but waiting for the next betrayal? People are who they are—let's start believing them the first time and not wait until it almost costs us everything.

Are You a Willing Contributor to Someone Else's Success?

Be a rainbow in someone else's cloud.
– Dr. Maya Angelou

Whenever I see a rainbow, I am so encouraged. For me, rainbows serve as a reminder of a promise, and they give me hope to believe that good things are on the way for me. Rainbows are so beautiful and come after the rain. At some point, we will all face the rain. Some of us may experience relationships that will fail. Some of us will encounter problems at work or in our businesses. Some of us will battle financial, emotional, physical, or mental sickness. When in our low season, we will need someone to walk with us on this journey of life. We will need someone to offer an encouraging word, make a phone call on our behalf, provide a listening ear, offer sound advice, or simply be there (whether tangible or intangible).

> *Rainbows serve as a reminder of a promise, and they give me hope to believe that good things are on the way for me.*

There was a season in my life when it appeared that everything that could possibly go wrong did. I felt so alone and as if things would never get better. I was so down and depressed that I cried every day. God sent me a rainbow. I had my

> *There was a season in my life when it appeared that everything that could possibly go wrong did.*

mother, her best friend, and a family friend who were the rainbows in my cloud. They were shoulders to lean on, voices of encouragement, and cheerleaders during the darkest moments of my life. They gave me hope to keep fighting, and assurance that I was a good person who simply encountered misfortune. They told me I possessed much wisdom and I should to continue to trust the voice which was inside of me. I can't imagine going through tough times without those individuals there to be the rainbow in my cloud.

In the years since, I have been the rainbow in someone else's cloud. I have shown up when others needed help. I have been there to sit with others when they were alone. I have provided references, ideas, strategies, and even jokes when others needed it. There is no greater satisfaction or joy I have found than when I have had the opportunity to be the rainbow in someone else's cloud. One day, I decided to send all of my "rainbows" flowers, unexpectedly, at their jobs. They were so happy and appreciative, but they had no idea how happy it made me feel. It was a small way to show them how much I valued them and the good things I wanted out of life just for them.

Who is your rainbow? Better yet, who considers you to be their rainbow? Go out and put a smile on someone's face today. Determine that you will not only show appreciation to your rainbow, but you will pay it forward and be the rainbow for someone else.

UNSTUCK. UNLEASHED. UNSTOPPABLE.

Accomplish What Appears to Be the Impossible Dream

It always seems impossible until it's done.
– Nelson Mandela

A black man could never be president. We won't see it in our lifetime. He did and his name is President Obama. Nothing good comes out of southside Chicago. It does. Michelle Obama is an attorney by trade and the wife of the first African-American president.

They will never reverse apartheid. They did. South Africa is not only free, but the man who would dedicate his life to the cause and reject offers of freedom would later become president.

The people who are saying "you can't" are terrified you will. It is your responsibility to show yourself that they are wrong.

They said Magic Johnson would die in a few years from AIDS. He didn't. It's been more than twenty years since he was diagnosed with the disease. Not only is Magic Johnson alive, healthy, and a business mogul, but he is an inspiration to many. The Bulls will never be better than the Pistons. They did and the Chicago Bulls would go on to win six championships and two three-peats. He will never be defeated.

She can't overcome cancer twice, but she did. She can't be a good mother because they are poor. She did, and all of her children are successful and have never been to jail.

He'll never be much of anything because he can't control his temper. Ben Carson would go on to become a gifted neurosurgeon.

Until it has been done, it will seem impossible. The people who are saying "you can't" are terrified you will. It is your responsibility to show yourself that they are wrong.

What dreams seem impossible for you? Remember, nothing (NO THING) is impossible with God.

 Have you ever seen someone accomplish something that you thought was impossible? Why do you think they were able to do so?

In Spite of What Others May Say, Your Past Does Not Define You; Unless You Let It

Don't look back. You're not going that way.
– Sharalyn Payne

It's quite easy to always wonder what could have been. What would have happened if we made that choice? Speculating or relishing on the past can cause us to not become excited and ignited about what lies ahead of us. Instead of anticipating the journey ahead, we begin to look at the past as either a monument of all that we can never be or as a memento of our past failures.

The problem with looking back is that the past is over, never to be relived again. No matter how bad or great it was, it is the past. To continue to look back is to question whether your best days are behind you and they are not. Your best days are in front of you (the days to come), and your future deserves a fair shot. You have the power to be even more successful than you were at the height of your past success in a different area, if you determine in your mind that success is yours for the taking.

Rest in peace; be comfortable with knowing that you made the best decision at the time with the information that you had.

Once it's over, it's over. You are not designed to become a slave to your past. You are moving forward and greatness is waiting on you to catch the revelation that your future is greater than your past.

UNSTUCK. UNLEASHED. UNSTOPPABLE.

I am reminded of the woman in the Bible (Lot's wife) who looked back and turned into a pillar of salt. Whatever you should have done, you didn't do it and it's over. It's in the past. Whatever you did and shouldn't have, it too is over. You are wiser now, and you have another opportunity to learn from the past and make better decisions. Rest in peace; be comfortable with knowing that you made the best decision at the time with the information that you had. I am not looking back, I'm looking ahead because that is the direction I am going—FORWARD! I will move forward.

Not too long ago, I was a speaker at a women's empowerment event. The event host introduced me, and she began to tell the women about a period in my life which was very challenging and hurtful for me. She thought it would be encouraging to the women. I had no idea that she planned to bring up that terrible moment in time. After the event was over, I needed to let her know that I had overcome that situation, that I was not defined by that experience, and it was certainly not something I wanted to live over and over. The experience happened. It was unfortunate. It made me stronger, better, and wiser. However, it was the past, and I refused to give the past power and control over me. I had rewritten the story and changed the ending. It was perfectly acceptable for those connected to me to use my past experience as a tool to encourage and motivate them, but I was not looking back. I had world problems to solve.

What experience in your past do you keep revisiting? Stop looking back and visualize your best days ahead, moving forward to your better place.

UNSTUCK. UNLEASHED. UNSTOPPABLE.

You Teach People How to Treat You

*Never make someone a priority
when all you are to them is an option.
– Dr. Maya Angelou*

How many times do we make someone a priority who makes us an option? We are all guilty of it. We answer when they call, aid in their rescue, and adjust our lives, schedules, and priorities to be there for them when they need us. Yet, if we need something from them or when we need them, they are never willing or in a position to help. We have made them and their needs a priority, and they have made us an option. We help them, sacrifice for them, and we are their "Ride or Die Friends," but yet we never receive the same consideration from them. We are left frustrated, hurt, and feeling rejected and abandoned, when we should simply understand the roles we play in each other's lives.

In reality, we teach people how to treat us. For years, we have heard "treat others the way you want to be treated" and while that is great, we never hear the flip side of it, which is everyone isn't taught the same thing. Treating others how we want to be treated can leave us vulnerable and with unrealistic expectations of others. I have been there to give others a place to stay when they didn't have one, to help others move at the last minute, to write resumes at the last minute when I was exhausted, to give solid advice based upon wisdom, to be the shoulder to lean on. All of that was great, as long as I was the one

I had to understand that I expected associates to be real friends. It was not fair of me to have wrongly categorized others and placed them in a position where they should not have been.

giving and making them a priority. What happened when I needed the shoulder to cry on? The same people I made a priority were the same people who had other priorities and were now too busy. My feelings were hurt.

I had to learn to modify my expectations of others. It wouldn't be easy because I truly believed that friends showed up. Friends helped when they didn't want to. Friends helped when it was not convenient. I had to understand that I expected associates to be real friends. It was not fair of me to have wrongly categorized others and placed them in a position where they should not have been. It was my lesson to learn that I chose to invest precious time in the undeserving and the unfaithful. I chose to make people a priority when they made me an option. Once I understood the impact of my choice, I caught the revelation that my life had value. I mattered, and I would not allow anyone to disrespect God's creation. He created me, and He did not create me to be used or abused. He created me to add value. It was up to me to determine who needed the value I had to offer and to use all of my resources wisely. I consciously decided I would be available for others who made me an option when it was not at an inconvenience to me. They did not have the power to change me to become a selfish individual. It would be very interesting when the people who had repeatedly not been there for me would tell me I had changed when I couldn't be there for them. They were right. I had changed. I learned to value myself. How freeing...

 Who are you making a priority when they are showing you that you are an option to them? Maybe it's time to adjust your priorities.

UNSTUCK. UNLEASHED. UNSTOPPABLE.

What Goals Are You Willing to Die Having Left Undone?

*Only put off until tomorrow what you are
willing to die having left undone.*
– Pablo Picasso

Where do you want to go? What do you want to do? Who do you want to be? What needs to be said? Who needs to be forgiven? When have you shown and told those you love and care about how you truly feel about them?

You see, there will come a day when life is depleted from us and when that day should come, we don't want to say that we wished we had taken the trip. We wished we had told our parents, friends, mates, and mentors what they meant to us and what value they brought to our lives. We wished we had run the marathon. We wished we had been strong enough to forgive those that hurt us. We wished we could have held our children and life partners a little longer and a lot tighter. We wished we could have left a positive legacy for our families, communities, and the world. We wished…

Stop putting off until tomorrow what you can accomplish today. If you don't want to say "I wish" if you died tomorrow, then it's probably a great idea to get busy today. I was saddened to learn that one of my childhood friends unexpectedly lost her aunt. When I read

> *Procrastination is the enemy of accomplishment. Procrastination pushes us further and further behind until one day, we give up completely.*

a letter from another member of her family reflecting on the loss, it was filled with all too many "wishes." It was simply heart-wrenching to read all of the goals and plans the two sisters had planned to do throughout the years, but never got around to doing them. We never know when our time will be up. We never know if we will again have an opportunity like the one that has been or will be presented. That's why we must take advantage of today and live as if it is our last shot at the opportunity of our lives. Procrastination is the enemy of accomplishment. Procrastination pushes us further and further behind until one day, we give up completely. My prayer is that when I expire, I will die empty. I will not have any tasks that are left undone.

 What goal can you not imagine dying and having not tried, began, or accomplished?

What Story Have You Created in Your Mind that is Not True and is Keeping You from Accomplishing Your Goals?

Fear is false evidence appearing real.
– Bishop G. E. Patterson

My former pastor and spiritual father would always say that fear is simply false evidence appearing real. I hate public speaking, especially when I cannot use my notes. However, for years it was an integral part of my role in corporate America. As an Organizational Development Consultant, I was required to equip C-level executives, senior leaders, and physicians with leadership skills. I remember getting ready to present to a room of over four hundred people who looked extremely different from me. The group I was presenting to had a reputation for being a very tough crowd. Although I had presented to large groups before, I began to feel extremely nervous. What if I forgot my presentation? What if they challenged me? What if they asked a question I could not answer? What if they refused to participate? I was bombarded by a thousand thoughts running through my head, none of which were conducive to the situation at hand. I had to pull myself together and change the story I

> *Unhealthy fear is designed to keep us from becoming the person we were created to be.*

was telling myself. I reminded myself that what I was feeling was not real. I was allowing the enemy of my mind to create a lie that I wasn't good at what I did, and that was furthest from the truth. I went to the lounge, collected my thoughts, and came out like the ROCK STAR that I was! Everything went better than I thought or anticipated. The reviews were positively amazing! People could not believe that I could present on that level and to that audience. My colleagues, who had acted like my enemies, asked for tips. You know you are good when your enemies genuinely sing your praises. I belonged in this arena.

Momentarily, I had allowed my fear to overtake my purpose. When I silenced my fear, I stepped into my power. Confront and conquer the fear, starting with the torment in your mind, and change the story you are telling yourself. Remember, whatever your fear is, it's simply not true. Unhealthy fear is designed to keep us from becoming the person we were created to be. We were created to reign.

What are you afraid of? What story do you need to recreate?

UNSTUCK. UNLEASHED. UNSTOPPABLE.

How to Recover from Disappointment

*Expect people to disappoint you and
you will never be disappointed.*
– Tony Perkins

One of my former clients (business partners) would always tell me to expect people to disappoint you and when they do, you will not be disappointed. If they don't disappoint you, then you will be pleasantly surprised. The Bible also directs us not to put our faith in man. How do you not put your faith in those you love or trust? For me, it certainly has not been easy. I want to believe the very best of others. I want to trust that what someone says he or she will do, will actually be done.

We are all human. As humans, there will be times in our lives that we will make promises that we can't keep or we shouldn't keep, for that matter. You've heard it said, "I'll always be there for you." Maybe, you will. Maybe, you won't…and maybe something will occur when you should no longer be there for me. Whatever the case, it's best that we remember that even well-intentioned people will forget.

> I don't believe that any of us wants to disappoint the people in our lives, but there are times when we cannot avoid the inevitable.

Things will come up that will cause people to disappoint us. Your spouse may forget your anniversary because they are overwhelmed with things at work. You may have to reschedule a date or a vacation with friends due to other priorities. You may not make it to your child's school function yet again, because you couldn't take the day off. You may miss another holiday with family because you can't get away. You missed a deadline because the computer crashed or you didn't receive all the data you needed in time. I don't believe that any of us wants to disappoint the people in our lives, but there are times when we cannot avoid the inevitable. We will disappoint others and we will be disappointed by others.

It may sound negative to expect people to disappoint us, but in actuality, it is both realistic and freeing. It can be a bit naïve to expect that people will be perfect all the time. Even the most loving mother or father will at some point disappoint us, even if it's just they didn't respond the way in which we wanted or needed at the time. When we understand that people will disappoint us, we free ourselves from disappointment, hurt, resentment, and negatively impacted relationships caused by us choosing to be unrealistic. We give ourselves and others the room to make mistakes and recover. We allow growth in the relationship because we become more resilient when disappointments occur and we choose not to live in a place of disappointment. Having said all of that, I will now say that we must choose how to proceed when the people in our lives continuously fall through on their commitments or neglect to live up to our expectations. In those relationships, we must calibrate and make a determination of how to address the situation. Clarity of expectations can alter the trajectory of the relationship.

For years, I had someone in my life that I really liked as a person, but she rarely did what she promised or committed. I could not count on her to follow through. For quite some time, I would be disappointed, expecting her to be where she was supposed to be, whether it was a lunch date or whatever. One day we were talking about her unreliable behavior, and she informed me that I had unrealistic expectations of the people in my life. Her comment hit me like a ton of bricks, and I immediately thought about the advice from my former client. I decided from that moment on I would allow people to be people. I would release others from any expectations that I might have while saving myself the disappointment in the event they were unable to follow through.

UNSTUCK. UNLEASHED. UNSTOPPABLE.

 How do you feel when you are disappointed by people? Who do you need to release from disappointing you?

UNSTUCK. UNLEASHED. UNSTOPPABLE.

Be Very Careful How You Handle Me

Never hurt your help.
– Bishop G. E. Patterson

Bishop G. E. Patterson was a wise man. He provided insight into my life. One of my favorite Bishop G. E. Patterson sayings was, "Never hurt your help." Have you ever had someone that you would have moved heaven and earth for? Have you ever had someone to whom you would have given your very last? Have you ever had that same someone betray or humiliate you? I know what it feels like to give your all to someone and the person who you gave your all to hurt you to your core. There was a man whom I was in a relationship with for an extended period of time. I had grown to care for him deeply. Not only was he my life partner, he was my friend, and I had a tremendous amount of respect and admiration for him. There is nothing legally or ethically that I would not have done for this man. I was "in it" and loyal to a fault. Imagine how I felt when I found this person whom I would have done anything for was betraying me while I was helping him. I stood with this friend, encouraged him when his world was falling apart, and walked with him through heartache, betrayals from business partners, extreme adversity, and devastating financial loss. While most had walked away when the money, celebrity, and power was gone, I remained.

Though standing by his side at his lowest point, this was the very person that pushed me away and cost me money, time, and heartache, and even made me question my self-esteem and values. It was as if he had determined to do everything in his power to bring me to the edge of sanity. I found out how close we can get to being pushed to the brink. It appeared as if this person was determined to destroy me. There are no words to describe the depth of my pain and despair when I found out how this person was hurting me emotionally, mentally, and physically. Although he never hit me, I would say that emotional and mental abuse can be just as real and painful. The difference is there are no identifiable scars to show.

A couple of years later this same person came back to me and wanted to rekindle the relationship that was irretrievably broken. He eventually came to see that I was a great friend and partner. I was supportive, loving, nurturing, and kind because I chose to be that way. When I declined the offer to rekindle the relationship, my heart broke for him. It was unfortunate that he had done too much to hurt his help. He voluntarily annihilated our relationship, friendship, and everything we had built. Though he was hurting, having buried the closest people to him, I just didn't have it in me to place myself in a position with a hurt person who refused to get help and take ownership for his destructive behavior. How do you recover when you have hurt your help? Sometimes the person you hurt may really want to be there, but the damage has been done, and you have to own the consequences of your actions. I just could not be there for him at the expense of myself.

> *Sometimes the person you hurt may really want to be there, but the damage has been done, and you have to own the consequences of your actions.*

 Who have you hurt that you need to go back and apologize to, so you won't hurt your help? If you have hurt your help, what lesson did you learn from hurting your help? Who has hurt you that you have helped? Are you willing to put yourself in the same position again?

No Matter Who You Are and What You Do, Not Everyone Will Like You

Twenty-five percent of people you meet will never like you; 25 percent of people you meet won't like you, but could be persuaded to; 25 percent of people you meet will like you, but could be persuaded not to; 25 percent of people you meet will like you and always be there.
– Joel Osteen

Everyone who knows me is simply in awe of the challenges I have often faced in corporate America. I am a true introvert, guided by my values, with a low tolerance for unethical or unprofessional behavior. I used to be amazed at my colleagues who chose to harass me or attempt to assassinate my reputation with no true knowledge of who I was or what I stood for. I have had people complain that I thought I was superior to them. When I asked for specific examples (because that wasn't my heart or my intention), my manager could not produce one example to substantiate the accusation. No matter how nice I was, no matter how I treated them, no matter how many times I tried to help and stepped in and saved the day, I still was not liked. Organizational leaders could sing my praises and nominate me for awards, but my manager would wait for months to tell me about it. She would often present my award after she presented someone else's award as well. Mine would always be an "I forgot all about this." It was so apparent that some of my co-workers would laugh about it. I just could not make them like me. One of the closest people to me is a former colleague who defended me without knowing me when others were talking about me. Since that day, we have been close, and I believe she is a person that cannot be persuaded not to like someone, no matter what anyone else says.

UNSTUCK. UNLEASHED. UNSTOPPABLE.

There was another company for which I worked and one of my colleagues so wanted to not like me. I would speak to her and she would simply ignore me. My colleagues and I would go to lunch together and she would talk to everyone, but me. One day, she stopped by my office and we had a really great conversation full of laughter. As we began to build a friendship, she revealed she didn't like me and had been rude to me over the course of the past year, all because she looked me up on the Internet prior to my first day with the company. Her research led her to believe I was small, pretty, and smart, and I was not going to come in the company making more than her friends who had been there for many years. Before I met her, she had decided she wasn't going to like me. Her closest friends thought very highly of me, but she just couldn't give in until my personality at the lunches got the best of her. She was persuaded that I wasn't so bad after all. Although we would both eventually leave the company, we continue to keep in touch and even find ourselves calling to invite each other to various events and functions.

I have a few people in my life that I liked as soon as I met them. Nothing you can say can convince me that they are not "good people." We may not be best friends or close friends, but I believe we will always be there for each other. I will always support them and defend them in the face of adversity because they are just solid people. I really believe they can't be convinced to not like me. When I heard Joel Osteen on television talking about this quote, I was freed to be me. It confirmed that no matter how hard I tried, I could not control how I was perceived or how well I was liked. My job was to not concern myself with trying to convince someone to like me. It was quite possible that they would never like me. Those who did would always be there, and I have found this to be so true. Sometimes we exhaust so much effort and energy in people who don't really matter in the grand scheme of things. It's time we nurture the people who matter and cultivate the relationships which sustain us.

 Who will always like you and be there for you? Start now to nurture those relationships. Who do you need to free yourself from trying to convince that you are worth liking? Free yourself now. Accept that no matter what you do, this person may never be persuaded to recognize you for the beautiful being that you are.

UNSTUCK. UNLEASHED. UNSTOPPABLE.

Do You Know Someone Who Is More Focused on Criticizing Others Than They Are with Improving Themselves?

Let the refining and improving of your own life keep you so busy that you have little time to criticize others.
– H. Jackson Brown Jr.

Have you ever been around people who are so preoccupied with the inefficiencies of others? Those people have no problem telling you everything that is wrong with you…yet, they will have a conniption fit if you even think to question one of their decisions. They can go on and on, pointing the finger at someone else when they are clearly not impacted by the decision, so why should another person's choices matter? I have learned that these are not the type of people I want close to me, because I am focused on making Sharalyn better. I have no time to waste evaluating someone else's decisions when there is so much work I need to do to make me better.

> *I have no time to waste evaluating someone else's decisions when there is so much work I need to do to make me better.*

I recall speaking with a former manager about the perception some members of the team had that I was "too professional, too buttoned up." (We were in leadership positions at one of the largest and most conservative financial institutions in the world. Go figure.) She proceeded to give me more conflicting feedback, which I listened to, processed, and compartmentalized when she couldn't provide concrete examples. At the end of the one-on-one, she asked my thoughts regarding the feedback she shared. I informed her that it was very interesting that people who hadn't worked with me and who had never met me had so much feedback to share regarding me. I also advised her I really wished I could find the time required to criticize and evaluate those who had no impact on me, my future, or my family. My spare time was spent adding value, enjoying life, and working to make me better. I was the youngest person on the team, the most educated and credentialed, and the only African-American. She laughed at my comment, although she knew I was serious. Her facial expression revealed she really didn't appreciate my remark.

> My goal is to not only be the best person I can be, but I want to leave those who come into contact with me in a better state after me than they were before they met me. People should not leave my presence and be in a worse state than prior to having experienced me. I add value.

I am 100 percent committed to becoming the best person I can be. My goal is to not only be the best person I can be, but I want to leave those who come into contact with me in a better state after me than they were before they met me. People should not leave my presence and be in a worse state than prior to having experienced me. I add value.

I remember encountering a young lady, beautiful on the outside, but she was the most critical and negative person that you could ever meet. It was as if she had a special talent or gift for criticizing everyone and pointing out other's faults to the point where it was difficult to be around her for more than three minutes. I really wanted to like her, but her attitude and viewpoints of others prevented me from spending any quality time with her. She was negative—a toxic bomb dedicated to destroying all who entered her presence. We were polar opposites in this sense. While I saw the best in others, she was laser-focused on identifying the worst.

I will never forget the time I was telling her about someone who did a lot in the community to help others, and how I was so happy this very successful person was so giving and grounded. She told me that he (this person she had never met and didn't even know his name) was probably only doing it to receive media attention. The individual I was speaking of had been actively involved in the community for well over fifteen years, with little to no media attention promoting his good deeds. She then began to tell me how I was "snowed" by individuals all the time. How could she know? I had only known her for a little over six months, and we spent very little time together. At that moment I could not resist asking her had she ever considered a job such as an auditor or inspector because she was truly gifted in identifying flaws, and we needed that especially in government-regulated industries such as healthcare. I went on to tell her that it wasn't that I was snowed, it was that I didn't have time to focus on someone else's life. I needed to focus on my own life. I couldn't fix someone else when I hadn't yet mastered fixing myself. You could cut the tension with a knife, and I simply allowed the silence to be uncomfortable. There was no need for a follow-up statement because I was not interested in a debate. I only wanted to shed light and allow her to make the ultimate decision of remaining in a negative state or choosing to direct her energy to self-improvement. Criticizing and revealing truth are not always necessary, nor are they interchangeable.

 Are you spending time criticizing or helping others? Why do you believe you have a license to criticize someone else?

UNSTUCK. UNLEASHED. UNSTOPPABLE.

Are You Dying Without Having Lived?

Twenty years from now you will be more disappointed by the things you didn't do than by the ones you did do. So throw off the bowlines. Sail away from the safe harbor. Catch the trade winds in your sail. Explore. Dream. Discover.
– H. Jackson Brown Jr.

There is something to be said for taking risks and living life on the edge. Now, don't get me wrong, I do value the consistencies of life as well. I just believe that life can be rewarding when you do some of the things that you want. The joy that comes with knowing you are willing to bet on yourself and do things your way is unexplainable. I have found that win or lose, I am worth the bet and more than likely, I win. The satisfaction of looking back over your life and seeing that when others would have been fearful, you displayed courage is fulfilling. What you learn about yourself and what you discover along the way about who you are and what you can achieve when you are willing to take risks is paramount to what you receive with a life full of regrets.

> *I have found that win or lose, I am worth the bet and more than likely, I win.*

Years ago, I wanted to relocate to a different city and delve into another profession. Many people had something to say about my decision to relocate to a city as a single woman with no family, friends, or support system. The decision to relocate was one of the best decisions I ever made. I learned how to be self-reliant, resilient, brave, embrace change, and how to

> *My greatest fear is dying without having lived.*

live by both instinct and faith. This challenge was out of my comfort zone. It was different for me, scary and exciting at the same time. I have been able to meet different people, explore other passions, and awaken other dreams and desires that I didn't know that I had. I have discovered things about myself that I didn't know were there and embraced other opportunities because I chose not to play it safe. I feel alive and determined to not die without having lived. When I look back over my life, I want to know beyond a doubt that I lived. I didn't always play it safe. My greatest fear is dying without having lived.

What are you waiting for? What is the dream that is in the bottom of your heart? If death knocked on your door tomorrow, what do you wish you would have done?

Five Simple Steps to Overcome Negative Thinking

I never looked at the consequences of missing a big shot...when you think about the consequences, you always think of a negative result.
– Michael Jordan

What you feed, you produce. It takes just as much energy to focus on the negative as it does to focus on the positive. So, why not envision yourself achieving the goal instead of failing or missing the mark? For some, focusing on the positive is harder because it's much like writing with your left hand if you are right handed. It can be the equivalent of using a muscle that you have never used before. Living in a positive state requires the conditioning of your mind. It means changing your thinking if you are not naturally wired to think that way. I have found that oftentimes, I get what I focus on. When I have worried myself sick about something, I ultimately received my very fear. Once I realized this truth, I decided that I would exert my energy in recalibrating my thinking.

> When fear or negative thinking would creep into my mind, I would search frantically, as if my life depended on it, for something positive to hold on to.

> When it's all on the line, when the outcome is huge, that's when it's even more important to envision yourself successful.

UNSTUCK. UNLEASHED. UNSTOPPABLE.

When fear or negative thinking would creep into my mind, I would search frantically, as if my life depended on it, for something positive to hold on to. When I began to put this into practice, I noticed that I felt better. I felt more optimistic, more grounded, and more grateful. I became more conscious of the people with whom I surrounded myself. The people who I spend the majority of my available time with know that I will not tolerate negativity on a regular basis.

I remember talking with someone about a project we were working on (which I was leading), and they gave me a million reasons as to why it wouldn't work. I was literally ready to scream. I finally had to stop and say, "Instead of us focusing on all of the reasons why this won't work, can we please just explore the one reason why it will work, and let's focus our energies on that instead?" I have neither the time nor the energy to focus on the negative. I do believe we should be aware of the obstacles and risks when making a decision, but after we have determined to accomplish a goal, let's stay focused on the accomplishment. I believe we must choose to control our thoughts instead of allowing our thoughts to control us. Focusing on the positive is necessary for success because the universe has a way of producing our expectations, whether our expectations are for achievement or failure. When it's all on the line, when the outcome is huge, that's when it's even more important to envision yourself successful. Too much is riding for you to be negative. Give positivity a winning chance.

I challenge you to:

1) Look for the positives in every situation.

2) Envision yourself joyful and successful.

3) See yourself accomplishing the goals you've set and work towards.

4) Snap a mental picture of yourself living in a continued state of peace and prosperity, and hold that photo in your mind.

5) Take it a step further, and place the photograph on the refrigerator as a reminder of who you are.

 What goal are you working on that is requiring you to shift your thinking?

UNSTUCK. UNLEASHED. UNSTOPPABLE.

Are You One of the Most Beautiful People in the World? Find Out Now.

You can't eat beauty. It doesn't feed you. These words plagued and bothered me; I didn't really understand them until finally I realized that beauty was not a thing that I could acquire or consume, it was something that I just had to be. And what my mother meant when she said you can't eat beauty was that you can't rely on how you look to sustain you. What does sustain us...what is fundamentally beautiful, is compassion for yourself and for those around you. That kind of beauty enflames the heart and enchants the soul. Get to the deeper business of being beautiful inside. There is no shade in that beauty.
– Lupita Nyong'o

> *I would like to know people appreciated my outer beauty, but what I really want is for people to fall completely in love with and cherish my heart.*

So often, we get caught up in how a person looks on the outside without taking a very close look at the person's heart. I, too, have spent money and time to look my best on the outside, but what about the inside? What type of person am I on the inside? Do I treat others the way I would want to be treated? Am I nice to only those who have the power or resources to advance my cause? Do I place more value on the external, the physical, than I do on the things that really matter?

UNSTUCK. UNLEASHED. UNSTOPPABLE.

I am so thankful that I have found what is most important in life. I have found that what makes me smile is being there for others. It is helping to make a difference in the lives of others in both tangible and intangible ways. I love to make others smile. It makes me feel good to contribute to worthy causes. To see the smile on other faces because I cared enough to help in a small way is definitely worth it.

I want my life to be a life known for deep love, impeccable character, integrity, gracefulness, kindness, and compassion.

I would like to know people appreciated my outer beauty, but what I really want is for people to fall completely in love with and cherish my heart. I want to be a person that cries when my friends cry. I want to be compelled to make a positive difference in the lives of others in any way that I can. I want to make you smile and make your heart dance. I want to be the person that moves you to make a difference, to be the kind of friend that supports you, who is just as happy for you when you win as I would be for myself. My mission is to be the person that visits the sick, who restores hope to the hopeless, and who makes random acts of kindness a lifestyle.

I want to be better, to do better, and to inspire everyone I come in contact with to be a better person as well. I want my life to be a life known for deep love, impeccable character, integrity, gracefulness, kindness, and compassion. In my opinion, that is real beauty. That's the type of beauty worth noticing and appreciating. A true love for others

When you give, not of your resources but of yourself, is when your inner beauty overshadows your outer beauty and you become beauty.

is stunning, appealing, and unusual. When you give, not of your resources but of yourself, is when your inner beauty overshadows your outer beauty and you become beauty. That kind of beauty cannot go unnoticed, for it enters a room and completely takes over. You know that someone beautiful has entered.

Have you ever met someone who was not what you would consider beautiful on the outside, but once you got to know them, their heart, and their character, they looked beautiful not only on the inside, but the outside as well? What happened? What characteristics did they possess? Now search yourself. Do you possess inner beauty—the type of beauty which cannot be extinguished?

UNSTUCK. UNLEASHED. UNSTOPPABLE.

How Do You Deal with Life Challenges?

*Don't wish it was easier, wish you were better.
Don't wish for less problems, wish for more skills.
Don't wish for less challenge, wish for more wisdom.
– Jim Rohn*

How true! This is one of my favorite quotes. For years, one of the things that I would have changed about myself was my temper. I am naturally nonchalant. I can be the nicest, sweetest person in the world as long as you are not pushing my buttons for an extended period of time or being extremely rude. If one of those things occurred, it was like I could go from zero to one hundred in a matter of seconds. It wasn't that I would hit someone, but I would let you know how I felt and what I thought of you (neither of which was necessary). I remember two of my less-than-stellar moments when I entered a verbal altercation with people I didn't know. From my perspective, I was spending my hard-earned money and I was being treated very unfairly. After numerous attempts to remain positive, cordial, pleasant, and negotiate the service I should have received anyway, I blew up on both occasions. In both instances, I let the person on the other end have it. Afterwards, I felt ashamed that I allowed another person's actions, no matter how wrong they were, to impact me and then choose to not walk away. I willingly participated

> *If I am to live the life I truly desire, I would have to fight for it.*

> *When life got hard, I had to do the hard work and draw from within, because challenges aren't going away.*

in the destruction of another person, and for that I was wrong. Both times my conscience and my heart demanded that I go back and apologize. On the second occurrence, I contacted my mother and discussed the possibility that I needed to seek professional help. I knew that I could not simply say that I wished that I could control myself. What if things got worse? I began to recite over and over that I was quick to forgive, slow to speak, and slow to anger. Although people may still irritate me, my response is now different.

There have been times when I have wanted to walk away and just give up on life because it seemed too hard. The only problem is that I am not a quitter. There is a lot of fight in me and a will to win. I have determined that some people have an easy life, and some people have a life filled with challenges. My life has been filled with challenges. The roads are different because the rewards are different. We have all heard it said, "To whom much is given, much is required." And there it is. My life for a while seemed filled with challenge after challenge after challenge. I had to come to terms that my life would not be smooth sailing. If I am to live the life I truly desire, I would have to fight for it. That meant I had to become better.

My attention had to be devoted to increasing my grit factor. I had to develop mental and emotional toughness, coupled with a positive attitude. I had to change my outlook and look for the positives in every situation. I had to swallow my pride and stay focused on what I wanted as the end result. When life got hard, I had to do the hard work and draw from within because challenges weren't going away.

What problems or challenges are you facing right now that require more skills? How can you become better in this situation? How can this situation actually make you better?

What Is the Reason People Come into Our Lives?

There will always be a reason why you meet people. Either you need them to change your life or you're the one that will change theirs.
– Madeline Sheehan

So often, we meet people and instantly try to figure out their place in our lives. We meet a sharp woman and we want to make her our friend. We meet a man and think that he could potentially be our lover or worse, our husband. We meet people at a networking event, and we want to make them our business partner or a contributor to our success. While the sharp woman could be our friend one day, she may be there to challenge who we really are. The man may be there to provide advice on a given scenario. The person you met at the networking event could be there to introduce you to someone else.

I believe we cross paths and exchange energy with people for a reason, which may not be readily identifiable.

I believe we cross paths and exchange energy with people for a reason, which may not be readily identifiable. Sometimes we may meet someone so that we may learn something from them, or we may teach them something. We may meet someone so we can connect that person with someone else who needs their knowledge or expertise. It could be that we meet the man or woman so we can be there during life's future trials or opportunities.

I can remember meeting a very tough woman who was an executive at one of my former employers. She has served many roles in my life. Living in a city with no family or close friends, she would invite me to spend holidays with her so I wouldn't be alone. She has been there to provide me with sound career advice on how to handle sticky situations. Because she is no-nonsense, there were people who would avoid and label her. I could have viewed her persona as a reason to avoid her, but she is a fun person to be around. She has introduced me to her family, and we have had been able to serve each other in various capacities. I have had people come and people go, but I am certain we served a purpose in each other's life—even if it was to make the person smile, laugh, grow, or introduce them to someone else.

One of the most fulfilling relationships I have had is the relationship with two women whom I consider to be my aunts. They are much older than me and one is my mother's best friend. My mother helped to rear one of my older cousins. When my cousin expired, my mother was in the process of developing a relationship with her now best friend who happened to be the age of my cousin. My mom often cites that she believes the reason she met her best friend was so that she could fill the hole left by my cousin. My mom's best friend is family and has been there for every celebration and obstacle that we have faced. I cannot imagine my life without her. She has helped to pull off surprises. She has given great advice. She has been an encourager. She has made me laugh until my sides hurt. She has been an angel sent from above.

Think about the people in your life who have come and gone. What do you believe was the reason for them entering your life? What purpose did you provide in their lives?

UNSTUCK. UNLEASHED. UNSTOPPABLE.

Does Money Change Who You Are?

*Money doesn't change men, it merely unmasks them.
If a man is naturally selfish or arrogant or greedy,
the money brings that out, that's all.
– Henry Ford*

I have seen it time and time again. Money has a way of revealing who you really are. Money illuminates your true self. If you are a giver and you come into money, you will find someone or a cause to give to. If you are a helper and you acquire money, you will find people to help. If you are a fool without money, you will be a fool with money acting foolishly. If you are selfish without money, you will be selfish with money. Money reveals who you really are. Money unveils your true character.

> *Money illuminates your true self.*

My mother is a very giving person. When I was younger, we had people to live with us until they could get on their feet. She would pick up people and take them to church, even when they lived in the opposite direction. She would buy food for those who had no money. She would purchase clothes for those who others would see the need and laugh or talk about. I lived in another state and had no idea what she was doing to help others. I found out about her mission to help others because one person was so grateful for what she was doing that they told someone else. When I asked her about it, she wouldn't confirm or deny, because she thought it was none of my business. When she received a large sum of money, she found

> *Money unveils your true character.*

those needing help and continued to do what she did all along—help others who were in need.

When a financially successful man I knew lost a large sum of money, I found that his true heart was ugly. As long as he had money, he was a giver and pleasant to be around. He was a great motivator and encourager. He wasn't perfect, and you could definitely catch glimpses of arrogance here and there. When he lost his money, he became a terror. He was mean, extremely rude, depressing, and one of the worst people to be around, often wishing ill will on others. He couldn't fathom that he wasn't the person on top. When he was able to climb back to the top, he became his happy self again. I believe the dark person he was without money was his true identity. The loss of money revealed his character, and his character needed much work.

Money should reveal that we are the same person with or without it. Hopefully, we become better with money and more appreciative and humble if we are ever challenged with concerns about money.

 What will the addition or subtraction of a large sum of money reveal about who you are?

UNSTUCK. UNLEASHED. UNSTOPPABLE.

How Do You View the Negative Experiences of Life?

It takes the same amount of energy to be positive as it does to be negative.
– Sharalyn Payne

Why focus on the negative when it takes the same amount of energy to be positive? Having and maintaining a positive outlook takes work, because we naturally want to talk about what is happening or what is going wrong. We can focus on the negative or we can focus on the positive, but we must understand that we attract the energy which we put out and focus our attention on.

> *If you want more positive things in your life, then focus your attitude and energy on looking for the positives in any situation.*

If you want more positive things in your life, then focus your attitude and energy on looking for the positives in any situation. It can be difficult at first and will require an adjustment in both your behavior and thinking, but it will be worth it. People may wonder what has happened to you, but you are changing and growing and setting the stage for great things to happen in your life. You will feel more in control. Positivity will repel negativity. As you practice this way of life and form better habits, be warned that you may outgrow certain individuals who would rather focus on the negatives and say that you have changed.

In the midst of negative situations, there are positive outcomes. My grandmother transitioned from this life unexpectedly, leaving me unprepared, but I am so grateful for all of the fond memories we shared.

UNSTUCK. UNLEASHED. UNSTOPPABLE.

We were not close at all when I was growing up. As a matter of fact, I never spent much time with her as a child. As I entered my college years, we became closer but never what I would call close. Our relationship matured and developed over the years. As a matter of fact, I loved my grandmother, but I often felt rejected by her. In spite of the rejection, I was determined to develop a relationship with her. So, when I learned that I wouldn't be able to see her again, I was heartbroken. I found myself wishing we had more time. We didn't, but I am grateful for the time we did have. I am appreciative that she did not suffer, but simply expired in her sleep.

> *In the midst of negative situations, there are positive outcomes.*

Through this, our family has become closer. I had the great honor of being the only grandchild to speak at her Celebration of Life service. At the repast, great speakers and broadcasters inquired about my speaking for a living. We all laughed because I would always joke and give speeches to my family on holidays while we were sitting around. People marveled at the beauty of the service, which she prepared and paid for years in advance. We were able to encourage others to prepare a will, ensure family members knew where important documents were located, and express our desires for details such as the celebration service, and so on. My grandmother's departure enabled me to spend time at home and see people that I had not seen in years, because I had not spent a solid week at home since I had relocated. Life happens to all of us. We will all have situations where we will struggle to find the positive. I am convinced there is a positive in every situation, if we look for it. Sometimes, we may have to look long and hard, but the positive really is there.

What are the positives in a negative situation you have faced?

UNSTUCK. UNLEASHED. UNSTOPPABLE.

What is Holding You Back from Getting the Love You Deserve?

Have enough courage to trust love one more time and always one more time.
– Maya Angelou

Have you allowed the opinions of others to hold you hostage from achieving your goals?

Have you ever met someone who vowed never to love again because they were hurt in a relationship or because the love of their lives transitioned into eternity? I was that person. I can recall going through a tumultuous relationship. The pain was so intense when it looked like we wouldn't work out. By the time we finally broke up for good, I felt as if I hated men with all my heart. The sight of men irritated me, because I felt like the person I gave my heart to insisted on abusing my love and betraying my trust. Men served as a reminder that I had made a bad choice. The man I gave my heart to was an unconventional hire, meaning I should have more closely evaluated my requirements and stuck to what truly worked for me. Instead, I chose to put someone in a position for which he was under-qualified. Because

> *The man I gave my heart to was an unconventional hire, meaning I should have more closely evaluated my requirements and stuck to what truly worked for me. Instead, I chose to put someone in a position for which he was under-qualified.*

of my poor choice, I gave away my power to love someone who would be more deserving of what I had to offer. I decided to step away from dating for an extended period of time until I could completely heal from my poor choice and not make another person pay for my bad decision. Now I can say I feel like I am ready to love again. I feel like this time will be different for me. No more bad hires, because I am now a better evaluator and interviewer when it comes to giving my love to someone.

It takes courage to love again when you have been hurt. To love again, when you thought you could never love another human being, is courageous. To put yourself out there and to be vulnerable to another person requires us to be a brave soul. Loving someone else with the possibility of rejection or betrayal can be tough, but if it works out, it is so rewarding. When we love, we are opening ourselves up to receive the greatest feeling ever known…love. It is such a great feeling when you know that you are truly loved and valued. To know that someone in the world cares about us and our well-being provides us with the ability to face life and move mountains. Loving another is a gift worth giving and a gift worth receiving. When you have been hurt, it takes power and courage to let go and trust yourself enough to know that you are ready to give and receive love again.

What is holding you back from being open to loving again? Open yourself up and get ready for true love. Trust that you have learned from your painful experience and you can love again. You now know what you are looking for and what you will and will not accept. You are courageous, lovable, and capable of loving.

UNSTUCK. UNLEASHED. UNSTOPPABLE.

How to Effectively Handle Your Haters

The ones who say you can't, you won't, and you shouldn't are probably the ones terrified that you will.
– Sharalyn Payne

Have you allowed the opinions of others to hold you hostage from achieving your goals? Have you allowed what someone else has said to you to keep you from going after your goals? When I was exploring the possibility of transitioning from education to corporate America, many people said that it would be hard. People said that I would not be able to enter corporate America without taking a huge pay cut because of the lack of experience I had in training adults. People said it would take years for me to be able to get a position that reflected my salary at the time. Some people even said I was unstable. It seemed they had a thousand reasons why I would not be able to successfully make the transition. When I make up my mind to do something, I can be pretty stubborn. It will take a lot to convince me that what I want to do is not feasible. When I decide that something is in my future, I am pretty determined to make it a reality, and I will allow no thing or person to stand in my way. Well, a funny thing happened. While volunteering for a non-profit organization, I met a lady who had recently relocated to the area and was a former teacher. She was also the former leader of training for a telecommunications company in Austin, Texas. While chatting about what Memphis had to offer, we connected because of our similar backgrounds and goals.

When I make up my mind to do something, I can be pretty stubborn.

UNSTUCK. UNLEASHED. UNSTOPPABLE.

In the middle of our conversation, she revealed her best friend was now the Director of Training for the organization of which she previously worked. She had been instrumental in securing her friend the Director of Human Resources role at that company, and they were now looking for someone to fill her former position. It just so happened that her friend would be in town to visit her that weekend. With that said, she then asked me if she could review my resume and give me some pointers and set up a casual interview with her friend at Starbucks that Saturday. We were moving fast! I remember wearing a white top with black capris to the interview, while the woman who would later become my boss wore shorts, a T-shirt, and a ball cap because she was going to the mall after the interview.

> *The funny thing is, the same people who doubted me and counted me out, now call and ask, "How did you do it?"*

A couple of weeks later, I was offered the position. They paid my relocation, gave me access to a company vehicle, credit card, quarterly bonus, and even a salary increase as to what I was currently making. Things worked out in my favor, and the naysayers then said that my tenure in corporate America wouldn't last. It's been ten years now, and I have never regretted the decision nor have I looked back. The funny thing is, the same people who doubted me and counted me out, now call and ask, "How did you do it?" I have realized that people will project their own fears onto you. They will try to hold *you* back because *they* don't have the courage to move forward. Sometimes, they don't want you to fare better in life than they do so they will plant seeds of doubt to hold you hostage from reaching your goals. When you know what you know about yourself, trust your gut, and let the naysayers fall by the wayside.

 Do you have someone in your circle that is scared you will surpass them? What are people saying that you can't do or won't do? Get them out of your ear now. Trust yourself, and the dreams and goals you desire for yourself, and prove yourself right yet again.

UNSTUCK. UNLEASHED. UNSTOPPABLE.

Strategies for Responding to Adversity

It is your reaction to adversity, not the adversity itself, that determines how your life's story will develop.
– Dieter F. Uchtdorf

If you desire to be a leader, a champion, or an achiever, then increasing your tolerance for adversity is necessary. As a leader, how you handle adversity is paramount to your success. When adversity comes, all eyes will be on you. Everyone will be looking to see what you will do and say. Will you crack under pressure or will you stay cool, calm, and collected? Your response to adversity will set the tone for those whom you lead. For years to come, they will tell stories about your leadership under pressure. Adversity will happen. It is a part of life. You cannot avoid adversity. If you are breathing, you will face adversity. Adversity shows you what you are made of, what you are truly about. So, it's not about what happens to you. It is more about your reaction to what happened. Your reaction impacts the outcome.

> *If you desire to be a leader, a champion, or an achiever, then increasing your tolerance for adversity is necessary.*

Because of my work ethic and positive attitude, I was recruited to work for my former boss when my company was taken over by another company. Although I liked working for this manager previously, he could not successfully transition to the new company's culture. Eventually, he simply retired on the job. So, when the company was looking to right-size, I was one of the ones caught in the crossfire when our entire team was eliminated. I remember receiving notification that I was going to be impacted. I was furious because I had spoken with my manager about the perception others had of our team and our outputs. Everyone was watching me. I could hear the comments and the whispers as I walked by. People who would normally not come around would meander around the area to see how I was handling the situation. My enemies, of course, were excited that I was being laid off. They could not wait to come and ask me what I was going to do next. With a smile, I would say, "Something better," or "Whatever I want to do," or "Move on to the next goal on my list." I made sure that I looked better than usual at work, and I plastered on my smile even though I was devastated initially. It was truly ridiculous, especially because I am a "never let them see you sweat" type of chick. I did not have time to focus on wailing and feeling sorry for myself. I had sixty days until my last day, and then I would receive a severance package. No one knew the layoff would be part of my success story.

I buckled down and set the following goals to keep myself focused and productive so I could make things happen. As long as I stayed focused, my emotions were under control.

Here are some of the goals I set to deal with the adversity:

Push Goal: Pocket the severance package and not to be out of a job for one day. (That meant I had to hustle to find my next gig.)

Goal 1: Be positive and not bitter about what happened; I didn't want that to come across in an interview.

Goal 2: Make looking for a job a game, and play the game daily until I won.

Goal 3: Become excited about the good thing that was about to happen.

Goal 4: Smile, even when you feel like crying.

Goal 5: Surround myself with sources of inspiration and motivation.

My last day at the job I was laid off from was the first day at my new job. The layoff paved the way for many blessings. I was able to retain the severance package, secure a more senior position, shorten my commute, and...earn more money, which is what I ultimately wanted. That opportunity also allowed me to meet some really great people who are still in my life today.

 What adversity are you currently facing for which you need to alter your reaction? What if your reaction to this determines the outcome and has direct correlation to the rest of your life?

UNSTUCK. UNLEASHED. UNSTOPPABLE.

What Happens When You Decide to Achieve the Big Dream for Your Life?

Dreams don't have deadlines.
– LL Cool J

Dreams don't have deadlines. One of my dreams is to travel the world. I want to be able to go when I want, with who I want, do what I want, and stay for as long as I want. For years, I would put off traveling and not go anywhere. I delayed my dream because I was waiting for the right people to join me on the adventure to see God's beautiful creation. As a creative, an inquisitive person, a dreamer, and an explorer, I desperately needed to see the world. I wanted to see the depths and the heights of this world. The dream of seeing the world began to burn from within. I knew that I could no longer quench the fire of achieving my dreams while waiting for the ideal situation. I set out and made a list of all the places I wanted to go. It was time for me to make my dream happen. I knew I could no longer delay my dream. Even if I had no one else to go with, I was going. I planned my trip, and I was so excited about my new adventure. While speaking with a college friend, the trip came up. She wanted to go with me. Great, I thought. Now, I wouldn't have to go alone. Months passed by, and she wasn't ready to book the trip.

I decided I was going anyway. I booked my

It doesn't matter if you are twenty-four or sixty-four, go after your dreams. It is interesting to find that when you begin to take steps to accomplish your dreams, the universe will support and bring resources along to help you.

trip and all of my excursions. My excursions nearly exceeded the cost of the airfare and hotel, but I didn't care. I was achieving my dream. My friend did go on the trip and we had a great time. Initially, she complained about the excursions, but when we got there, she was blown away. We often talk about how that was a trip of a lifetime. We had a blast! Since that time, I have continued to travel to each location on my list. I feel so accomplished when I check off each exotic locale, one by one. I actually look forward to sitting down and planning where I'm going next.

There are no words to describe how it feels to accomplish one of my dreams and how proud I feel that I decided not to wait on anyone to participate in my dream. This dream was important enough for me to achieve with or without another person. When I made the decision to go solo, someone came along with me so I wouldn't have to do it alone. It doesn't matter if you are twenty-four or sixty-four, go after your dreams. It is interesting to find that when you begin to take steps to accomplish your dreams, the universe will support and bring resources along to help you. It's been years since I took my first trip to another country. Although I don't mind traveling outside of the United States by myself, I've only made one solo trip to another country (since I decided to just go for it).

 What dreams have you delayed? Dreams don't have deadlines, so it is never too late to get started. It is a nightmare to die without having tackled your dreams.

UNSTUCK. UNLEASHED. UNSTOPPABLE.

How Do the People in Your Life Make You Better?

*You are the average of the five people
you spend the most time with.*
– Jim Rohn

Who do you spend your time with? It's an important question because your relationships are vital to your success. What if I told you that I could determine where you will be in the future by just watching who you spend the majority of your time with? If we are the average of the five people we spend the most time with, then that is major. Someone once said, "If you show me your friends, I'll show you your future." I am extremely particular about who I spend my time with. If you spend your time with family-oriented people, you are probably family-oriented. If you spend your time with spiritual people, you are probably spiritual. If you spend your time with broke people, you are probably broke. If you spend your time with successful people, you are probably successful. Like attracts like, meaning we are often attracted to people who reflect our dreams, visions, and goals. If you spend time around negative people, you are probably negative. If you aren't already negative, then you will probably become negative.

> *If you show me your friends,
> I'll show you your future.*

> *I would suggest if we want to achieve epic success, then we need to get away from people with our problems and get around people who have our solution.*

UNSTUCK. UNLEASHED. UNSTOPPABLE.

I would suggest if we want to achieve epic success, then we need to get away from people with our problems and get around people who have our solution. If you want to be happily married, then why would you spend your time with people who speak negatively about their spouses or their marriages? If you want to be successful, then why hang around people who are content with living beneath their potential and outside of their purpose?

Begin to create the life that you want by altering who you spend the majority of your time with. When you are around people, you are learning and picking up their habits. I'm not saying that you need to isolate yourself from others who don't have what you want. I'm saying you just don't give them all of your time. Think about it like this: What can your broke best friend who you spend all of your time with teach you about creating wealth? What can you friends teach you about accomplishing your dreams if all they talk about is fear? How can you learn how to run a successful business if you never consult entrepreneurs or those skilled in developing businesses? Whatever you want out of life, begin to spend the majority of your time with those who have already accomplished what you desire.

When I wanted to increase my faith, I spent time with those who were faithful. Subsequently, my faith increased. My belief level went up. I began to see my dreams accomplished. When I desired wisdom, I sought out those known for providing sound advice. Now, my inner circle looks to me to provide advice on a number of topics, and my opinions are valued and respected. I became the person I wanted to be by purposefully selecting those who I would devote my time.

Who are you spending too much time with? Who do you need to spend more time with? If you don't know five people who have what you want, then it's time for some networking.

UNSTUCK. UNLEASHED. UNSTOPPABLE.

The #1 Key to Getting What You Want and It Has Nothing to Do with Action

Stay on Faith Street. If you want a new car, why do still have your old car sitting on bricks in the driveway?
– Steve Harvey

I firmly believe in the power of expectation and faith. If whatever I am looking for didn't happen today, then I am looking for it to happen tomorrow. You must make preparations for the very thing that you desire. If you are a farmer and need rain for your harvest, then by all means, shouldn't you walk around with an umbrella? Your actions should line up with what you believe.

> *You must make preparations for the very thing that you desire.*

One Memorial Day, my aunts visited me, along with my mother, sister, and brother-in-law. I went to the grocery store and purchased plenty of food for us to eat for breakfast. I thought I was purchasing enough for breakfast for one day. When I returned home, one of my aunts was up and asked me if she could cook breakfast for the family, which was perfectly fine by me. When we were ready to eat, we saw that she didn't cook everything and we were still hungry. One of my other aunts went into the kitchen and cooked more food. The aunt who originally prepared breakfast said we are saving that for tomorrow and we had enough. We certainly didn't think so. We were still hungry.

> *Your faith is a seed and the accomplishment of your seed is the harvest.*

UNSTUCK. UNLEASHED. UNSTOPPABLE.

The next day, we went to the grocery store again and bought food to grill for dinner. Well, what were we thinking? The aunt who cooked breakfast the day prior thought once again that we bought too much food and was irritated that we were cooking it all. I had to explain to her that we didn't lack the resources to buy the food, nor were we living beyond our means. There was no need to ration out the food. In my house, we save money, invest money, but we also live in the overflow. I have an expectation and deep-rooted belief that I will never go without and that I will always live an abundant life.

Man would consider me successful, but I am expecting even more. I am expecting to have food to give away to those in need. I am expecting to be able to feed thousands, even millions, one day with my resources. When I began to share my vision, everyone agreed. They were excited and started speaking positivity and blessings over their own lives. Your actions must line up with what you believe. While I am not advocate for being wasteful or living foolishly, I certainly don't believe in embracing a lifestyle of scarcity.

If you are expecting a great husband, why hold on to the trifling man who doesn't respect you? When I decided that I wanted to relocate, I sold my home (which was like a retreat), in expectation that I would be relocating in another state. I had not yet applied for an opportunity, nor spoken with anyone about relocating, but I believed that it would happen and soon. So, I had to prepare and make ready for what I wanted to happen. I had to believe it, see it, prepare for it, and expect it.

Within three months of selling my home, I was in another state, working in my new career. If you want to be a size six and you are a size sixteen, go and buy a couple of size six dresses.

Stop holding onto what doesn't work because of fear, and expect that you will accomplish your dreams. Start acting like you already have it. Activate your faith by making preparations for it. Remember, we reap what we sow. Your faith is a seed and the accomplishment of your seed is the harvest.

UNSTUCK. UNLEASHED. UNSTOPPABLE.

 What do you want? What do you need to get rid of to make it work?

UNSTUCK. UNLEASHED. UNSTOPPABLE.

The #1 Self Destructive Behavior That Can Ruin Your Life

Never judge someone's movie based upon a few scenes, highlights, or previews. Some people are just better actors than others.
– Sharalyn Payne

We have all been guilty of this at some point. We look at celebrities and think they have it all. We think they should be happy. We think that they don't have the same problems as us. We think if we could just trade places, everything would be all right. So, when they commit suicide or overdose, we are left in shock, wondering what happened because we know that if we had all that money, our problems would go away. If only we knew. If only we knew the depth of their pain and struggle, we would appreciate our personal struggles.

I have a good friend who, in the past, would always measure her marriage to what she thought she knew about the relationships of others. This was based upon what she saw looking from the outside. She would look at the relationships of others and compare her relationship to theirs, often falling into a state of depression or resorting to harassing her husband. Someone else was happier because they were holding hands in public, or someone's husband truly loved his wife because he always doted on her and complimented her in the presence of others. She thought I had nice furniture because my ex-beau purchased it for me. I was often taken aback as to how she could draw such huge conclusions based upon what she thought she saw.

She was in disbelief when I told her that I purchased the furniture myself. I sacrificed and had no furniture when I relocated back home until I saved enough money to purchase exactly what I wanted without charging it, financing it, or going into my savings account. The couple she thought was extremely happy really wasn't. It took her friend telling her on her death bed about how her husband was a serial cheater. Then, she began to appreciate her husband. She began to see that her husband treated her like a queen. As far as she knew, he was a great provider. He was her friend. He was faithful. While he wasn't as affectionate in public as she would have liked, he was faithful. While her friends displayed a happy marriage, life began to reveal they weren't really happy at all. They simply were aligned at presenting the image they wanted the world to see.

People show you what they want you to see and tell you what they want you to know. No one ever really knows what is taking place in another person's home or life because only a fool reveals everything. We have all heard, "fake it until you make it." Sometimes, we need to act happy until we become happy. We need to act loving until we feel loving. If we measure our lives and happiness based upon what we think we know about the lives of others, we will be sadly disappointed to find that so often it's smoke and mirrors. We all have highs and we all have lows. Some of us choose to not give in to our feelings or speak about the giants we are facing. We slay the giants in secret. We walk around in pain, hoping that no one can see how we really feel. We laugh when we want to cry. We give the appearance that we are living, when we are secretly dying. Because we are great actors, others are destroying themselves trying to get where they think we are.

Whose highlight reel are you watching and comparing it to your own movie? Were you able to also view the deleted scenes and the alternate ending? Remember, the director tells the story he or she wants you to see from his or her perspective. The characters give the script life.

UNSTUCK. UNLEASHED. UNSTOPPABLE.

How Does Your Partner Treat You?

Never fall in love with someone who treats you like you are ordinary.
– Oscar Wilde

I am a lover of love. I love being in love, seeing love, and showing love to others. Love is a precious commodity. I cannot wait to meet the man who falls in love with me, and I fall in love with him. In the meantime, I am very careful now about who I will allow myself to fall in love with. Falling in love with someone who does not value me and cherish me is completely out of the question. Falling in love with someone who doesn't respect me like a queen and treat me like a princess is not an option. As his queen, I want my partner to value me, consider me, and respect my ideas. I want my partner to see me as an intricate part of his life. I want him to treat me as if he can't see himself without me. I want him to go out of his way for me. I want him to be the man who would love to put a smile on my face when things are unfavorable. I want him to be someone who tries to make my sad moments better. As his princess, he treats me like he would treat his daughter. He protects, provides, and would do anything in his power to make life easier for me. He wants the best for me and is my cheerleader in life, vowing to always walk with me along the way.

> *Falling in love with someone who does not value me and cherish me is completely out of the question.*

> *A man who treats me like I am ordinary just won't do because ordinary is easily replaceable.*

UNSTUCK. UNLEASHED. UNSTOPPABLE.

I want a man that I view as a man worthy of love, respect, and admiration. I want to treat him as extraordinary because he really is. A man who treats me like I am ordinary just won't do because ordinary is easily replaceable. We don't place a lot of value on ordinary, until it's gone. The extraordinary are things we cherish, protect, and treat with care. I am an extraordinary woman who treats my man as if he is extraordinary and irreplaceable. I require the same of my partner, and I am willing to wait for it because I know I am worth the wait.

How does your mate treat you? Is this treatment good enough for you?

UNSTUCK. UNLEASHED. UNSTOPPABLE.

What Would Happen if You Devoted More Energy to Achieving Your Dreams?

There's a one degree difference between hot water and steam. Turn it up.
– Antonio Adair

> The one-degree difference is what separates the winners from the champions.

The one-degree difference makes all the difference. Hot water is produced at ninety-nine degrees Celsius or two hundred twelve degrees Fahrenheit. Water boils at one hundred degrees Celsius, which then produces steam. Steam can actually power a train, whereas, hot water cannot. The one-degree difference is what separates the winners from the champions. The extra degree is the difference between people who manage teams and those who transform teams. The one-degree difference separates the six-figure earner and the millionaire earner. The one-degree difference is what separates the Michael Jordans, the Lebrons, the Steph Currys, and the Kobes from those who ride the bench. The one degree is the extra step you take when others would be content. The one degree is deciding that good enough is not enough. The one-degree difference is when you have achieved your dream of making it to the NBA. The off-season rolls around and instead of relaxing, you are working

> The one degree difference is what separates the Michael Jordans, the Lebrons, the Steph Currys, and the Kobes from those who ride the bench.

with your trainer daily. You are working on the areas you need to strengthen. You are making your strong even stronger. You are watching the replay tapes. You are eating healthy. When you come back, you are stronger. You are fiercer. You got better. You stepped up your game and you do it over and over again. Your name will go down with the ages. You decided to turn it up and now little kids look up to you. People want to be like you. You are a brand and because you turned it up, you have given others hope for what they, too, can accomplish.

Do you want to accomplish your goals? Put in the extra effort required to make it happen. The one-degree difference could be what you need to catapult you into a different level of success. The one degree is where legends are made. The one-degree difference is where success stories are born. The one-degree difference can change the trajectory of your life. I challenge you to work harder than ever before. I challenge you to train better. I challenge you to love stronger. I challenge you to push harder. We often hear to give it 110 percent, but the one degree makes all the difference. So, if you have been giving it 110 percent, it's now time for 111 percent. The additional degree can open doors that you never thought possible. The additional degree can totally change your life forever and take it from great to outstanding! The additional degree can propel you to even greater success. Go ahead and give it a chance.

 What are you doing *good* already that you need to put in a little more effort to accomplish the results you desire faster?

UNSTUCK. UNLEASHED. UNSTOPPABLE.

Do You Wear Out the Tough Situation, Or Does It Wear Out You?

Tough times never last, but tough people do.
– Robert Schuller

What do you do when it seems like the bottom is falling out of your life? What do you do when it appears that everything that can go wrong does go wrong…and all at the same time? What do you do when it appears that life has been designed to break you? How do you keep your head up when your dream becomes your nightmare? You decide that you must fight for your life. You embrace the reality that you are resilient. You tell yourself that you are a survivor. You will fight and win. You tell yourself that you are a warrior. A warrior is one who fights back and wins. Warriors win battle after battle. You find peace and comfort in knowing that after the rain comes a rainbow. You remind yourself that spring always comes after winter. Nothing in this life is permanent. Everything is subject to change— even the seasons of our life. One of my favorite people in the world says it like this, "There are five seasons. Winter, spring, summer, fall, and due season." Due season comes after we have gone through a tumultuous period in our lives, and we are due to receive all of the good things we are

> *Though it may appear that the hard season or the drought will last forever, it won't.*

> *Success is not easy, and the ride can be both rewarding and hard at the same time. If we are not mentally tough, it can break us.*

waiting on. We are due to accomplish our dreams because we have put in the work. We are due for the season of the tough times to change and yield way for the times that bring us great joy.

Fall will always come after summer, and winter will always be followed by spring, and spring will always be followed by summer. What I am trying to say is that just as there will always be seasons in the natural, there are seasons in our lives. Some seasons will be longer than others, but at some point the season has to shift. Though it may appear that the hard season or the drought will last forever, it won't. The challenge is reminding ourselves that what we are going through is temporary. It is learning to become mentally tough. The fact of the matter is, often the season is there to develop us and prepare us for the next season. Many of us want to experience great success. With great success comes many challenges. Success is not easy, and the ride can be both rewarding and hard at the same time. If we are not mentally tough, it can break us.

We won't always have a down or rainy season. The sun will come out again in our own lives. There are cycles and seasons, and we can go crazy if we don't understand that what we are experiencing today is temporary and will not last forever. Hang in there and stay in the fight. Do not check out on life, because another season is coming if we remain steadfast. Being mentally tough requires you to have hope and faith even when it appears there is no end in sight. It requires you to make up your mind that you are a winner and your willingness to do whatever it takes to not only endure the season, but learn from it. Being mentally tough requires focus and not giving into your feelings. Tough times are temporary times and cannot destroy the hopes and dreams of tough people.

 How tough are you? What are you facing now that requires you to recalibrate how you view the situation?

UNSTUCK. UNLEASHED. UNSTOPPABLE.

Do You Have True Friends and More Importantly, Are You a True or Fair-Weather Friend?

I define my friends by who is there in the highs and lows of life.
– Sharalyn Payne

> A friend will support you, look after you, be there for you, share in your joys as well as your sorrows.

The words "friend" and "love" are two words which are often abused and used carelessly. There is a statement in the Bible about friendships that I find rather interesting. It says that a friend sticks by you like family. I believe that I have associates and people that I am a friend to, but not many people who I would define as a friend. It's not that I don't like the people I associate with or I can't trust people. I define a friend very differently from most people. I simply define a friend as a person who will stand and walk with me during my successes as well as my failures. Friends are with me when things are going well as well as when things are at the worst. A friend will support you, look after you, be there for you, share in your joys as well as your sorrows. A good friend will tell you when you are wrong in love and will "cover" you when needed.

> A friend is a tremendous responsibility and a lofty honor.

A long-term acquaintance has a best friend who is truly like his brother. Through the years, I have admired their friendship. I have witnessed them be there for each other in so many ways. They have provided inspiration and encouragement to each other. They have been there for family events, even having Sunday dinners together. They are so close that their immediate and extended family considers each other as family members as well. These two have supported each other through triumphs as well as devastating financial losses. What I love about their relationship is that they are respectful of the friendship and each other as individual men. While they may not agree with each other's decisions, they respect each other and know when to speak up and when to back down.

I can recall when one member of the friendship made a poor decision. It seemed that everyone who knew of the decision had something to say. One day in particular, there were some people discussing the decision in the presence of my acquaintance. When my acquaintance was asked of the decision, he just looked and asked very sarcastically, "Why?" The way in which he asked why let everyone in the room know to let it go. When some inquired about the decision a few months later, this time he stated that it was a rumor and a speculation, and that he needed "to just let that go." All along, he knew the information to be true because his friend had informed him as soon as the decision came back to bite him.

These two have negotiated business deals on each other's behalf and walked away from other deals because they had faith in the other's gut intuition. Imagine how happy they were when the deals worked out. They speak highly of each other in the absence of the other. That is what I would call a true friend!

A friend is a tremendous responsibility and a lofty honor. A friend is not a role which should be taken easily or entered into lightly. It requires work and sacrifice to be a friend, but it is so rewarding. During the darkest moments of my life, a friend's love is what sustained me and gave me the will to keep fighting. At my lowest, my mother's friends as well as my family encouraged me, walked with me, prayed for me, wanted the best for me, and believed in me. One of my greatest achievements is that I can call various people and ask if I am a friend and receive a resounding YES, followed by, "I'm sorry, what did I do?" While being a friend requires the ability to be selfless, genuine, and loving, true friends do not go unnoticed. I believe we should take the time out to let our friends know that they are loved and appreciated.

 Are you a true or fair-weather friend?

UNSTUCK. UNLEASHED. UNSTOPPABLE.

How Long Are You Willing to Pay for Someone Else's Offenses?

Resentment is like drinking poison and then hoping it will kill your enemies.
– Nelson Mandela

After experiencing a horrible breakup with the person who I thought was the love of my life, I felt like I would never be able to love again. Secretly, I wanted him to disappear from the face of the earth, and I wanted absolutely nothing to do with dating. I made up my mind to be perfectly content alone and even wanted to have a hardened heart regarding relationships. That just wasn't me. It isn't in my core to hate. Like most people, I have endured my share of heartache, pain, and disappointment. I have experienced blatant and hidden racism. I have been mistreated in relationships, passed over for promotions, and even had some people try and tarnish my reputation by spreading mean, vicious lies. I have seen people do their very best to plan my downfall, and others who said they were my friends to turn their backs on me when it wasn't favorable to be seen with me. In spite of all of those situations and even more, I

It is much more rewarding to use the weapons designed to make me resent my enemy as a tool for me to take a closer look at my heart.

Holding onto resentment kills you, and you die a slow, agonizing, lonely death while the other person freely goes on living life like it's golden.

have found myself not being able to drink the fatal poison of resenting a person who is helping to mold my character and prepare me for promise. I have found that it is more damaging to my enemies to smile even when hurting and let them wonder how I truly feel. It is much more rewarding to use the weapons designed to make me resent my enemy as a tool for me to take a closer look at my heart.

I remember when the person who was supposed to love me was determined to break me. Some of those who loved me and wanted the best for me couldn't understand why I didn't hate him and why I refused to tarnish his reputation. For me, it simply wasn't worth it. Resenting him would eat away at my core and prevent me from being able to give and receive love. Resenting him was the equivalent of sentencing myself to life in prison and throwing away the keys, which was far worse than a death sentence in my opinion. I could not allow the negative experiences of one person to have that much control over me. I needed to live, and living requires forgiving over and over again. Only I could take back the keys of my life and open the door to the prison cell. Staying one hour in a prison cell where I didn't belong was far too long. Holding onto resentment kills you, and you die a slow, agonizing, lonely death, while the other person freely goes on living life like it's golden. When you resent others because of how they have treated you, it's like they commit the crime, but you do the time.

 Who do you need to forgive? What do you need to let go? Remember: You have the keys to the prison cell. Open the door and walk out.

UNSTUCK. UNLEASHED. UNSTOPPABLE.

Are You for Sale?

Too many people spend money they earned…to buy things they don't want…to impress people that they don't like.
– Will Rogers

To be delivered from people is freeing. Being confident in who you are without needing validation from others takes courage. Every year, you see it around Christmas. You see people who don't have the courage to stand for how they would like to be treated, give in to the pressures to "play nice" for one day. What about being nice all the other days of the year? Retailers make a ton of money because people go out and spend money to buy gifts for people they don't necessarily care for, let alone love and respect. The Christmas season is the time that my coworker who has plotted against me all year, buries the hatchet for a day and buys me a gift, only to go back to their same manipulative ways the very next day.

> Be definitive about what you want, when you want it, and why you want it.

I recall working at a job, and my manager was horrible. She was untrustworthy, prejudiced, uninterested in me as a person, unsupportive, displayed obvious preferential treatment, and tolerated unprofessional and unethical behavior. Every year, she would send a Christmas present. Initially, I sent a gift as well. We were playing nice, right? One day, I made up my mind that I wasn't doing it anymore. I was no longer willing to perpetuate disrespectful behavior. I wasn't going to contribute to Boss's Day for a boss that didn't deserve anything in my opinion. I wasn't buying Christmas presents for team members with whom I didn't have a great relationship. I wasn't going to allow anyone to pressure me to spend money that I worked for on anything that I didn't want to. (Oh, well.) I'm sure you have seen it too. Some people buy houses and cars to impress others because they want others to believe they can fit in, are superior, or to make them think they have arrived. It's truly sad when they are deep in debt and still not validated by the people they so desperately want to impress.

Be proud of who you are. Be definitive about what you want, when you want it, and why you want it. The people who love you will love you whether you have a nice car or an old car. They will love you if you live in the suburbs, and they will love you if you live in a box. So, you might as well do what you want with your money. Even if it means living a meager existence to be a blessing to someone else who needs it, because helping others and not impressing others is what life is truly about. If you can only receive conditional love because you are spending money or because you give the illusion of success, then it's probably time to re-evaluate the people and relationships in your life.

What have you purchased or are considering purchasing to impress someone else? Do you want it because it is your heart's desire or are you purchasing it to impress someone who really isn't worth it? Love and acceptance are never for sale and can never be purchased.

What Would You Accomplish if Your Talent Was Backed by Hard Work?

Hard work beats talent when talent fails to work hard.
– Taras Brown

I have met so many people who were much smarter and sharper than me. They were poised to be much more successful than I, and accomplish far greater. I am astonished that our lives turned out completely different. What happened? We had access to similar resources. To be honest, on the surface, it looked like they actually had better resources—two parents in the same household, both with professional careers, money to invest in their children's dreams, and a host of other supporting cast members (family and friends). So, what prevented these seemingly talented individuals, who looked like they had it all, to not reach the pinnacle of their success? What has kept these talented individuals with so much promise from maximizing their potential? Knowing these individuals and taking a look at their lives, from what I can see ,from my limited view, it happened because they didn't work hard. They had the talent but failed to put in the work.

> *The truth of the matter was that I didn't want to achieve the goal badly enough to put forth more effort.*

> *Hard work, coupled with talent, can take us places that we could never have dreamed of otherwise.*

UNSTUCK. UNLEASHED. UNSTOPPABLE.

Even in my own life, I must admit that I could have accomplished so much more if I would have worked harder. I remember there were some goals I wanted to accomplish, and I could have had I been willing to put in the work. I was talented and capable of achieving the goal. Yes, I did some work, but did I really give it my all? I didn't. I know I could have done more. The truth of the matter was that I didn't want to achieve the goal badly enough to put forth more effort. The idea of accomplishing my goal didn't outweigh the effort needed on my behalf to put my work with my talent.

Talent is not enough. Talent gets us in the game. Hard work, coupled with talent, can take us places that we could never have dreamed of otherwise. There are many talented people who are lazy. Hard work can overshadow talent, especially when talent doesn't work hard.

 How can you develop your talent? What can you accomplish if you combine your talent with hard work?

UNSTUCK. UNLEASHED. UNSTOPPABLE.

Are You Letting a Lack of Vision and Creativity Hold You Back from Living the Life of Your Dreams?

Take a good situation and work on making it great.
– Marcus Brittmon

So often we look for the perfect person and pass a lot of great opportunities and people by because they are not wrapped in the package that we want. We miss our knight in shining armor because we are looking for the perfect situation. We pass up job opportunities because they are not offering exactly what we want.

> *Don't pass on a good opportunity because it does not come packaged with all the perks you believe you are entitled to.*

I am not an advocate for settling under any circumstance. However, I am an advocate for understanding the perfect situation for you and how it will fall into your master plan. I am not perfect by any stretch of the imagination. I am not looking for a perfect man to enter my life so we can live happily ever after. My future partner is not and will not be perfect; however, he will be perfect for me. We will complement each other instead of compete with each other. Our relationship with two

> *Don't let the desire for perfection hold you back from the satisfaction of promise.*

imperfect people who love, honor, support, and respect each other will have the potential to become great...if we stay focused on our purpose for being together and focused on our relationship goals.

What if I choose a partner who is not wealthy, but financially successful and decent with money? I can take the good situation which is a financially successful partner, combine it with altering my lifestyle and spending habits, investing our money properly to make it grow, and the result will be a great situation. My partner may be perfect for me and may have most of the other qualities I desire, but lack in this one area. I can partner with him, be a great support system, and we can make choices together that will position us for long-term success.

The same holds true regarding a job. Don't pass on a good opportunity because it does not come packaged with all the perks you believe you are entitled to. It may be that you need to accept the position, pay your dues, and do your very best while you're there. If you'll accept this position and be faithful while there, it can open future doors for you. It may be possible that what you need, you'll learn while there. Who you may need to connect with to lead you to the perfect company or opportunity may be at the company that you want to pass on. The things that we want to pass on because we are waiting for "perfect" may be the building blocks for the opportunity that is to come. You have the power to take lemons and make lemonade, lemon cakes, lemon pies, and so much more...or you can become a sour lemon later because you lacked vision and creativity. Don't let the desire for perfection hold you back from the satisfaction of promise.

What situation can be improved if you changed your perspective and committed to viewing the opportunity as a blessing and treating it as such?

UNSTUCK. UNLEASHED. UNSTOPPABLE.

How Strong is Your Foundation When It Has Been Shaken?

Forgiveness is a decision, but trust is a construction.
– Bishop T. D. Jakes

You choose to forgive. Just because you choose to forgive someone doesn't mean that it's wise for things to automatically go back to the way they previously were. Trust is a construction. That means it has to be built. To build trust means that you have to do something for the relationship to work. It is acknowledging what happened and making a conscious decision that you are willing to do the groundwork necessary for the relationship to be restored and successful.

> *Just because you choose to forgive someone doesn't mean that it's wise for things to automatically go back to the way they previously were.*

Understanding that trust is a construction requires both parties being willing to work on rebuilding. Just because you choose to forgive doesn't mean that you should blindly give back trust. Forgiveness doesn't require you to act foolishly.

Think of it like this: If you let someone live with you and when you left, they decided to steal all your valuables, would you continue to allow them to stay there without locking everything up? Would you require they leave when you leave, or would you give them the key with full reign and access to your home, knowing that they are a thief? I don't know about you, but it would depend on the person before I would determine if they could ever enter my premises again. I'm not so sure I would ever allow them to be in my home again without me being there to closely supervise them, because I wouldn't want to have to lock up my valuables because someone is there that couldn't be trusted.

I remember being friends with someone who wronged me. I loved her dearly, but she showed me clearly that she had no interest in re-establishing trust. She was more interested in sweeping everything under the rug and acting as if nothing ever happened to damage the relationship. Because she couldn't acknowledge her wrong and slowly take the steps necessary to rebuild the friendship, the result was that, although she was forgiven, I couldn't readily trust her. How would I know that she was truly sorry for her actions and understood the impact her actions had on me? How would I know that she was truly interested in preserving the relationship because it was valuable to her? I had to move on because I saw that it takes time to build a house and the foundation has to be solid. The same thing holds true when rebuilding and repairing any relationship. If the relationship is worth its salt, then it will be tested. The test is that when someone has wronged you are they willing to put in the work needed to repair the relationship. The big question is, are you willing to be patient during the construction process and understand that you could have a beautiful product in the end if you invest in the relationship as well?

Remember, sometimes it's okay to forgive and move on. Other times, it is necessary that you observe a person's actions and look for the genuineness in their heart, accompanied with actions, that shows they want to rebuild the damaged relationship. If the person is unwilling to rebuild the relationship after they have wronged you, or if you are unwilling to rebuild after you have wronged someone, then why continue the relationship instead of cutting your losses? If the person and the relationship are worthy of your forgiveness, then you should be willing to build a road back to happy, considering you were instrumental in the deconstruction of the relationship.

 Who have you forgiven, but neglected to require them to work on repairing and rebuilding the relationship? Why? Is it because you feel you are unworthy of requiring someone to work to restore the relationship?

Be honest with yourself. How does that make you feel? What is the true status of the relationship? Do you want a brick house or a straw house? Doing the work determines how secure the relationship really is. Don't fool yourself.

Do Your Friends Deserve You and Do You Deserve Your Friends?

If you go looking for a friend, you're going to find they're scarce. If you go out to be a friend, you'll find them everywhere.
– Zig Ziglar

One of my proudest accomplishments is that I have learned how to be a good friend—a true friend. I know how to be there to offer encouragement and support, to give a good laugh, to just be there. I know how to be happy for my friend's achievements and partake in their success just as if it were my own. I know how not to allow anyone to disrespect my friend, whether or not they are around. I know when to tell the truth, how to state the truth, and when my opinion is simply irrelevant and does not need to be voiced at all.

> There may be times when we are to be a true friend to someone who can do absolutely nothing for us, because our blessings will never come from them.

It is often said a friend in need is a friend indeed. Some people simply don't know how to be a friend. They haven't seen the example. I have watched my mother maintain friendships with several women throughout my entire life. These are women with character and integrity. Women whose lives exemplify their values and what they say. They have been there in the good and bad times. They may not talk every day or every month, but they have proven to be friends. To have a friend, you must be a friend. Friends give the advantage, they don't take advantage. Sometimes, we have unrealistic views of our friends. I probably have been guilty of this. During the process of building a business and writing a book, I have needed friends for support. I have needed friends to provide a listening ear to a chapter or a blog post. I have wanted those who I wanted to believe were friends to show up to support my events. I was hurt and even deeply disappointed when I learned that the very people I supported would not support me. Some wouldn't even return a phone call. It was astonishing to learn that people I had supported through the years with time, money, and advice wouldn't be there for me at all. For some of my "so-called" friends, I had supported everything they had invited me to if I was in the city, physically and financially. So, to say I was disappointed was an understatement.

I do believe that the experience was necessary for me to realize that for so long I had been a friend to those who were not worthy of my friendship. I was "unequally yoked" in friendships of which I should have been a distant acquaintance. I was busy being a friend to people who probably didn't truly understand what it meant to be a friend. We had completely different definitions of friendship. Because I failed to get the proper understanding and be honest with them (as well as myself) about what friendship actually looked like, I was disappointed. Perhaps, I had unrealistic expectations of my friendships. Nevertheless, these experiences taught me to treasure more where I expended my valuable resources, including the most precious resource of all—my time.

I no longer expend my energy where it is not wanted or appreciated. I now understand the value of my friendship and I am, in turn, limiting my time with people who only want to receive the benefits of my friendship but not be a friend. I do know that there are people that I am supposed to be a friend to, who are not necessarily supposed to be a friend to me. That's okay with me. It's just now I am more cognizant of the purpose of the friendship. Sometimes, our friends are there to grow us instead of give to us. There may be times when we are to be a true friend to someone who can do absolutely nothing for us, because our blessings will never come from them. In that case, I believe we are sowing good seeds for which we will reap the benefits of later.

UNSTUCK. UNLEASHED. UNSTOPPABLE.

 How have you shown that you are a friend? What is your definition of friendship? Are you worthy of the good friends you have in your life?

UNSTUCK. UNLEASHED. UNSTOPPABLE.

Go, Be Great

*You have untold strengths and resources inside.
You have your glorious self.*
– Sue Monk Kidd

We spend too much time focusing on and studying others, instead of using the same energy to focus on and learn ourselves. We were created on purpose for purpose. There is something that we were placed on this earth to do that no one else can do. I remember sharing my vision with someone who was in a position to help me. Instead of receiving encouragement, I was asked the question: "What makes you think this has not already been done?"

Well, I never said that what I was working on had never been done before. It would be absurd for me to think that. Everything has already been created. There is nothing new under the sun. However, the way I would do it and my unique skills, background, and perspective would be different. Apple didn't invent the cell phone or the camera. Apple changed the way we use our cell phones. Wendy's and McDonalds didn't go out of business when White Castle sold cheeseburgers and neither did the Mavericks because the Grizzlies got a franchise team. There is room for everyone. The key to your success is to decide that you will go be great. The key is to use your untold strengths and resources placed inside of you and not let them go to waste. It does no one

> *We spend too much time focusing on and studying others, instead of using the same energy to focus on and learn ourselves.*

> *If you will take the time to uncover your hidden assets and find a way to maximize your potential, then you can experience joy, satisfaction, and fulfillment that you never thought possible.*

any good to bury your talent, your strengths, and the resources placed inside of you. Discover your strengths, increase your value, use your strengths to your advantage. If you will take the time to uncover your hidden assets and find a way to maximize your potential, then you can experience joy, satisfaction, and fulfillment that you never thought possible.

How do we identify our strengths? Spend time thinking about what you do well. What are you complimented on, and what are the things that people rely on you for? When you do what you do, what effect does that have on others? How do you feel when you do it? Spend time with yourself and get to know yourself. I know myself quite well. I know my strengths, limitations, fears, and passions. I know what I am great at, good at, and what areas can be improved. With all that I know about myself, I know there is so much more that I don't know about me. There are still treasures to be unearthed and stories yet to be told. I constantly ask God to reveal my strengths and resources and to help me to see myself the way that He sees me. I pray I will fall in love with that person. For now, I will work on making my strong stronger and finding a way to use my strengths to make a difference.

What are your strengths? Who are you? How can you leverage your strengths to improve the world in which we live? If you don't know your strengths or are uncertain, it's time you found out. Get busy, for your future depends on it.

UNSTUCK. UNLEASHED. UNSTOPPABLE.

Why Is Time More Precious than Money?

Time is more valuable than money. You can get more money, but you cannot get more time.
– Jim Rohn

Over the years, I have lost a number of loved ones. People who were very close to me and others who weren't as close, but who had more impact and influence over my life. The pain was so deep because I valued the person and the relationship. So, to have to say goodbye knowing that I would never see the person again on this earth was tough, even heart-wrenching. Death has a way of putting things in their proper place. Losing friends around your same age is extremely difficult because you are forced to face your own mortality. You never really think in your youth that people your age, whom you have grown up with, will die. I came to understand that I can gain more money, but not more time. Losing them totally changed my perspective on life. I became more aware of how I was living. I no longer lived in fear or bondage, because I became aware that I was running out of time.

> *Death has a way of putting things in their proper place.*

Time is a commodity that we can never purchase more of—we can only leverage time. We all have the same twenty-four hours in a day. However, we each choose to spend our time differently. I am protective of my time. I am on time and have very little patience for those who try to control or dominate my time. Family and friends often laugh because they know that if you are more than a couple of minutes late, and you have not informed me that you will be late, I will leave if I have something else that I could be doing at that moment. My belief is that I can never get the time back that I am wasting by waiting. There are other things that I could be doing. You cannot pay me enough for my time and being late on a regular basis is a character issue. I believe that if you are habitually late, you think that you, your time, and what you had to do is more important than keeping your time with me. (In some extreme cases, you may even think you are superior.) If people come to meetings unprepared or are distracted, I reschedule the meeting so that we can function in the highest and best use of the time at hand. Other than that, we are wasting time…precious moments that we will never get back again because no one can ever turn back the hands of time.

In my personal relationships, one of the things that I value most is quality time. I love spending time with those that I care about. Rarely do I desire a physical gift. I cherish the time the person chooses to spend with me because I know that in that time we are creating memories, precious moments that we can reminisce and reflect on later, but never get back again.

Who do you need to spend more time with before it's too late? How can you be more respectful of your time?

UNSTUCK. UNLEASHED. UNSTOPPABLE.

How Do You Show the People You Love That They Are Loved?

Love is in the details.
– Oprah Winfrey

How true! Love really is in the details. Think about receiving a gift. How do you feel if you just are given the gift and it is unwrapped? What if it is placed in a gift bag? What if the gift is wrapped in a beautiful box? Are you oozing with anticipation? Well, I love to show people that I care about them, and I believe that love is in the details. It's not enough to just ensure that my family eats dinner. I love to set the table with fresh flowers and have music playing in the background and serve a home-cooked meal prepared from scratch. I like to prepare the plates and relish in our time together. Love is going the extra mile, going out of your way to ensure that another person can feel and see the love you have for them because they are worth it. Every single detail matters and is never too much when you love. Details show that the person is worth it. When I go all out for those I love, I am even more excited than the person receiving the gift. I'm doing it to put a smile on their face and make them feel super special, but the love that it gives me to see them happy is more fulfilling than anything else in that moment. What I receive in return makes all the difference.

> *Love is going the extra mile, going out of your way to ensure that another person can feel and see the love you have for them because they are worth it.*

 How has someone shown you they loved you? How do you show someone you love them? The details matter, because the person matters. I often thank God for being concerned with every single detail of my life because one thing I know for certain. God loves me and was concerned about the details when He created me.

UNSTUCK. UNLEASHED. UNSTOPPABLE.

How Badly Do You Want to Be Successful?

Success is hard work, discipline, determination, and dedication.
– Coach Danny Joe Young

There is not an easy path to sustained success. To be successful, to accomplish one's goal, requires a healthy dose of hard work, discipline, determination, and dedication. My coach, Danny Joe Young, would often say success is more hard work, more determination, and more dedication. I would think Coach Young knew what it took to achieve success. As the coach of East High Lady Mustangs, Coach Young led the team to seven state titles, fifty-seven individual state titles, as well as regional, city, and district titles. Coach Young had more wins than any program in Memphis history. To be successful requires a commitment to follow through even when you are tired, feel defeated, or even want to give up. Success requires you having the ability to walk away from some things, to evaluate choices that will propel you forward, take you backward, or leave you stagnant. Success requires a sheer determination that you will do what it takes to make your dreams come true. The road may become difficult, you may grow weary, and sometimes you may even wonder if the end result is truly worth it. Deep down you know that it is. You know there is no other option for you, but to be successful.

When you really want to be successful, you will roll up your sleeves and get it done. This one quote has stuck with me for over twenty years. Success isn't easy and doesn't come to the weak. It requires

> *Success isn't easy and doesn't come to the weak.*

true commitment. Whether it's a successful career, marriage, family, or business, you must decide that you will work hard at it, determine that you will stay committed to seeing it through to the end, and know going in that there may be times when you may want to quit, but you will not quit until you accomplish your goal. I can remember wanting to win at track and cross country, but sometimes I wanted to quit. There were times when it was so hot outside when running that I wanted to quit. I did not want to have to go to practice another day in the heat, but I wanted to win. I knew that if I quit or didn't give it my all, it would be impossible for me to win. The will to win demanded that I show up and give it my all. I have taken that same work ethic throughout my life. I do my best not to commit myself to any activities that I'm not willing to give it my all. I believe with all my heart that I am supposed to be successful in everything that I do. Failure is never an option.

What do you want to succeed at? Are you practicing the success principles of Coach Young or are you doing just enough to get by? Are you determined to make it work and give it all you've got? Are you dedicated to your success or are you half in and half out?

UNSTUCK. UNLEASHED. UNSTOPPABLE.

What Does Your Name Say About You?

Your name should mean something.
– Bishop G. E. Patterson

My mother and my late pastor would always say your name should mean something. I can hear it over and over again. When we were contemplating building a new church, my pastor was able to take out a multi-million dollar signature loan because his name meant something. The creditors knew that he would not renege on the loan. They knew that he would accomplish what he purposed to do.

When I was a child, my mother told me that she was going to spank me. Days passed by and I thought she forgot. I thought I was in the clear. When we got home from church about five days later, she kept her word and she spanked me right before I was going to sleep. Before she spanked me, she told me that she kept her word and that if she told me she was going to do something, I could count on it because she wouldn't make me a promise that she wouldn't keep. Boy, was I upset!

> If you make a promise or a commitment, then you should follow through on what you said you will do.

Decades later I still hold the same belief—your word should mean something. If you make a promise or a commitment, then you should follow through on what you said you will do. Some people think I am too passionate, some think I am too rigid, and it's all because I carry myself a certain way. I expect for those in my inner circle to handle me a certain way as well—it's called self-respect. Life is precious and we only get one shot at it. So, I don't allow people to treat me any way they'd like and think that it's okay. If you tell me you are going to do something, then I expect you to follow through. I don't believe it's in good character to hear your name and think that it is synonymous with a liar, a cheater, or someone who doesn't follow through.

Life is precious and we only get one shot at it.

When people hear your name, what do they think of? Do they envision a successful person, a tough person, a nice and kind person, a ruthless person, a gossiper, a liar, an adulterer, a cheater, a man or woman of character and integrity, a selfish person, a maverick, or a visionary? What is synonymous with your name? How you carry yourself, your actions, and your associates all determine what someone thinks about when they hear your name. I want my name to mean something. When people hear the name Sharalyn, I want them to think of a lady with character and integrity, who is confident, loyal, smart, and sharp. I want them to think of me as a visionary, a giver, a woman after God's own heart, a good friend, and a lover of family. I want them to recognize me as someone who is focused, balanced, fun, funny, humble, a person with high moral standards, dependable, supportive, kind, and a person who holds them accountable. Because my name means something, I strive for perfection, understanding that I will never achieve perfection, but that I can be the best me that I can be. People may attempt to destroy my name, but those who have had the opportunity to spend time with me know who I am, what I stand for, and what I can be counted on for.

 What does your name say about you?

UNSTUCK. UNLEASHED. UNSTOPPABLE.

What Have Your Failures Taught You?

It's fine to celebrate success, but it is more important to heed the lessons of failure.
– Bill Gates

I have learned from my successes, but I've learned so much more from my failures. My failures have served as a refining experience and while the tuition was expensive, the education was invaluable. Failures have taught me humility, grace, mercy, and decisiveness. I have learned whether or not I truly wanted something, and my failures allowed me to explore the motive behind the desire. I have been able to determine how badly I really wanted something and whether or not I was willing to put in the hard work required to win. Failure was bitter, until I realized that if I learned from the lesson, then I really didn't fail after all. Failure bred grit...determination, tenacity, toughness, persistence, and resilience. Failure exposed who was really there for me—who was in my corner cheering for me to get back in the game. Failure showed me if I had it in me to get back up and reinvent myself or

> *Failure showed me if I had it in me to get back up and reinvent myself or exposed if I was going to sit on the sidelines defeated because things didn't turn out as I expected.*

> *If you are a warrior, a person who fights and wins, you will look at failure as an opportunity to improve your strategy so you are not in the same position the next time you battle.*

exposed if I was going to sit on the sidelines defeated because things didn't turn out as I expected.

Failure was cold, hard, bitter, and brutal. It was a feeling that I never wanted to experience again. The pain was so debilitating that I had no choice but to do everything in my power to study it, to pay attention to it, so I would never have to learn its hard lesson again. The lessons of failure required introspection and retrospection. I could either play the tape of failure over and over again, or I could shake it off, learn the lesson, and keep pushing forward. The most important lesson failure has taught me is that I may have failed at a particular event, but that doesn't define me or make me a failure. Only two things make me a failure. The first is not trying at all, and the second is failing to get back up after a disappointing loss, allowing it to torment my spirit and soul. If you are a warrior, a person who fights and wins, you will look at failure as an opportunity to improve your strategy so you are not in the same position the next time you battle.

 We have all experienced failure. What have you learned from your failures?

UNSTUCK. UNLEASHED. UNSTOPPABLE.

Are You a Sure Thing?

*I don't like to gamble, but if there's one thing
I'm willing to bet on, it's myself.*
– Beyonce

I am not a gambler at all. The funny thing is I have gone to the casino with a couple of my friends and, as long as they give me their money to play with, I can win thousands of dollars for them. Whenever I have taken out my own money, I lose. I don't understand it, but I am wise enough to know that is a huge sign that I do not need to gamble.

> I know that I am a fighter and not just a fighter, but I am a warrior.

The exception is that I will always gamble on me. I know me. I know that I am a fighter and not just a fighter, but I am a warrior. I will to win. I do what others aren't willing to do, which gives me the advantage. I work hard and I play hard. I study the task at hand and prepare to win the game. I visualize victory and I am hungry for success. I put in the work. I focus. I know how I perform when the odds are against me and my back is against the wall. I know and live the principles necessary for success. I block out the opposition, the critics, the naysayers, and even the negative

> The odds are in my favor, not because of who I am, but because of who He is.

voice in my head. I will always bet on me…because I know it's a sure thing. The odds are in my favor, not because of who I am, but because of who He is.

 If you were betting on yourself, would you be willing to put it all on the house? Are you worth the gamble to yourself? If you wouldn't bet on you, then why should someone else?

UNSTUCK. UNLEASHED. UNSTOPPABLE.

Do You Underestimate Your Value in Relationships?

We need to teach our daughters the difference between a man who flatters her and a man who compliments her. A man who spends money on her and a man who invests in her. A man who views her as property and a man who views her properly. A man who lusts after her and a man who loves her. A man who views himself as a gift to women and a man who believes she's a gift to him. And then we need to teach our sons to be that kind of man.
– Unknown

A man did not make me, so a man cannot validate me. The right man created especially for me can affirm who I am in his life and together we can achieve purpose. He can build me and support me, but he can't determine my worth or my value. There is a difference between a person complimenting you and trying to flatter you. Flattery can be deceitful and is not always meant to be genuine or truthful. Spending money is a nice, thoughtful gesture, but investing in my future is priceless and will take me farther than any purse, car, or diamonds ever will. I remember when I was building

The right man created especially for me can affirm who I am in his life and together we can achieve purpose.

I know beyond a shadow of a doubt that I have value and something to offer myself, the man I am supposed to be connected to, and the world.

a business. It was very interesting to see the men who wanted me to believe that they were so into me, but who were unwilling to invest in me or my dreams. They would be willing to take me to dinner, but wouldn't even offer me any advice to help me see my dreams come true. Needless to say, these weren't the men I would be remotely interested in. I can take my own self to dinner. So, what value do you bring to my life? What value do you see in me when you look in my eyes?

I know beyond a shadow of a doubt that I have value and something to offer myself, the man I am supposed to be connected to, and the world. I understand that long after the gift, no matter the material value, I have worth and can help the right man to prosper even more. I'm not moved by a man with potential because potential is unearthed action. I am attracted to a man of action, who is a builder and an executioner. A man who views me as property feels that he owns me and can do with me as he chooses, including getting rid of me when he no longer sees value or sees something that looks a little better. Viewing me properly means knowing that I am a woman, seeing me both as a lady who deserves respect and his lady, who he cherishes, treating me like a queen, and protecting me emotionally and physically like his princess. The man for me will understand that he has the power to shape me. He understands that I am a gift to him. He is blessed because I am in his life. I have his back, and I am in his corner. He recognizes that because I am connected to God, his prayers are answered and he obtains favor with God. Who wouldn't want the favor of the Lord? Although he admires my physical beauty, he knows I am a treasured gift worthy of his love, time, and attention, and not just his body. He knows that I am worth the wait. He knows that the ecstasy we can share when we are in love cannot be compared to the few minutes of pleasure shared outside of a loving, healthy relationship. Because I value me, I require him to respect me and a real man always will. Only the real men will step up.

 How do you view yourself? How does the man or woman in your life treat you? What are you teaching your children verbally or otherwise regarding how they should be treated by the man or woman in his/her life?

UNSTUCK. UNLEASHED. UNSTOPPABLE.

How Does Controversy and Challenge Define You?

The ultimate measure of a man is not where he stands in times of comfort and convenience, but where he stands at times of challenge and controversy.
– Rev. Martin Luther King Jr.

> Some of us would not have survived if we were born into slavery or the Civil Rights era.

I truly believe that God knows when we should be born in this world. Some of us would not have survived if we were born into slavery or the Civil Rights era. My mother has said that I would have been dead had I been born during that era. Currently, America is going through what looks like a civil war. The Black Lives Matter movement and the killing of black youth by police officers are causing an uprising, and we are in a state of emergency. You have celebrities speaking up, risking their careers, to weigh in on the matter and fight for change. You have others who would rather remain silent and be comfortable, rather than risk losing fans or sponsors. In 2016, we were on the cusp of electing the first female president of the United States of America and part of her platform was that she has made things better for the less fortunate for a vast majority of her life—even when faced with those who opposed her tactics and her affiliations.

> I have been persecuted and ostracized for standing up for what's right.

More than once, I have been the victim of racist and unjust behavior. I have been persecuted and ostracized for standing up for what's right.

UNSTUCK. UNLEASHED. UNSTOPPABLE.

I've watched others put their head down and act as if nothing was happening because it wasn't happening to them. I've had co-workers and friends say that while they knew that what was happening was wrong, it wasn't worth the risk of them losing their jobs or families because they got involved. It was just easier to accept that the maltreatment and behavior was a part of life. Some were so afraid of what might have happened by them even voicing their opinion in private, that they wouldn't discuss the situation at all, even years later. Their choice to not get involved doesn't make them wrong; we all have different gifts. Theirs is one of survival rather than courage or risk-taking.

I refuse to stand by and allow injustice to happen on my watch. I will stand up and fight for what I believe in and let the chips fall where they may. I have lost some relationships because I am willing to stand up for what is right when others will sit back and accept injustice to get along and protect their jobs, careers, and reputations. While I respect their decision, I do not accept that as part of my life. I will take the risk to see a better today for those who come after me for causes that matter to humanity. For me, standing at times of challenge and controversy is part of my DNA. I was designed and created this way for a reason. It is not acceptable for me to allow unacceptable social norms to continue in my presence and I sit by idly. I believe there are times when we must stand for right and suffer the consequences. Our ancestors and leaders fought to allow us to partake in certain liberties, and I will not allow their sacrifices to be diminished or forgotten. My character is at stake.

 Take an assessment of the world around you. Is there something going on in your life for which you need to stand up or address? What worthy causes can you lend your time or money, but more importantly, your voice, to make a difference for someone else?

UNSTUCK. UNLEASHED. UNSTOPPABLE.

Are You Living Your Goals or Someone Else's?

Big goals get big results. No goals get no results or somebody else's results.
– Mark Victor Hansen

I live by goals. I cannot wander haphazardly through life hoping good things will happen. I've got to set some goals for myself. I've got to be a willing participant in my own success. Successful people set goals. It's not enough to simply set goals, but it takes faith to set big goals. When you set those goals, if you want the goal badly enough, then your subconscious mind will go to work for you setting the right things in place for you to get the very thing that you want. The same holds true when you don't set goals. When you neglect to set goals, you receive the very thing that you want for yourself, which is nothing. What's worse is that you will find yourself achieving the goals that someone else has set for you, which normally is connected to their own goals.

> *I've got to be a willing participant in my own success.*

I urge you to set goals for yourself, if you haven't already done so. Determine what it takes to achieve the goal. A goal is a dream with an expected date of actualization attached to it. A goal without a target date is only a wish. I knew when I entered grad school that I wanted to be finished within one year. I wasn't just there to take classes. I was there to get what I needed to further my career.

> *It is a great sense of accomplishment to be able to look and see what I have accomplished through God's favor and grace.*

I had to structure my courses in such a way that allowed me to meet my goal. I am constantly setting new goals, evaluating my goals, and redefining what I want for myself and not what someone else wants for me. I have huge goals, which seem larger than life. I know that it will take a massive amount of work and major favor, among other things.

Setting both short-term and long-term goals has worked out for me. It is a great sense of accomplishment to be able to look and see what I have accomplished through God's favor and grace. I don't take it lightly or for granted. I am humbled that I even have the ability to set goals, because that in itself is a gift that some people never get to experience.

What are you waiting on? What are your short-term goals? What are the things that you need to accomplish within the next ninety days to six months? What are your long-term goals? What are the things you want to see accomplished within the next three to five years? What wheels do you need to set in motion to achieve your goals? Are these your goals or someone else's goals?

UNSTUCK. UNLEASHED. UNSTOPPABLE.

How Big Are Your Goals?

Whatever you're thinking, think bigger.
– Tony Hsieh

I write my dreams and thoughts down on paper and revisit them often. I am often reminded of I Corinthians 2:9 (NLT): "No eye has seen, no ear has heard, and no mind has imagined what God has prepared for those who love him." To me, that means whatever I can think that I want, God wants so much more for me. I want to be a great wife. God wants me to be even better than that. Perhaps he may even want me to teach classes to other women on how to be a great wife, igniting a movement of women who transform the world through their families. I desire to make a positive impact on my community and country. Perhaps I am called to make a positive impact on the world globally and for generations to come. I want to be a giver. God desires me to be a philanthropist. I want to be a mother. God sees me as a mother to generations. I want to be a successful entrepreneur. God wants me to be a mogul. And you know what? I want for me what God wants for me and that is His best.

> *I need to start thinking bigger, dreaming bigger, and praying bolder.*

> *Small goals don't impress God, for they don't always require His help.*

I need to start thinking bigger, dreaming bigger, and praying bolder. Even as I am typing right now, something even bigger is brewing. As I was thinking about one of my goals, God just placed an idea in my head to even expand on that idea and take it to another level. Small goals don't impress God, for they don't always require His help. Big goals require the assistance of someone else. Bigger goals demand that God intervene for them to materialize. Expand your vision. Think bigger.

No, bigger. No, even bigger. A little bigger. Push a little bit more. Okay, now believe that you will see your "bigger" goal come to pass.

 What is it that you want? Now, supersize it. I dare you to maximize it.

UNSTUCK. UNLEASHED. UNSTOPPABLE.

Have You Ever Suffered So Greatly That All You Could Do Was Pray?

*When the world pushes you to your knees,
you're in the perfect position to pray.*
– Rumi

I have gone through some things that, at the time, I thought I would never recover from. You couldn't have convinced me that I would have made it through the pain. The journey felt unbreakable as if it was designed to push me over the edge. I had fallen into utter despair and there was no way I could have made it through the refining fire without God. He alone could help me. Yes, I had people praying for me, because sometimes the weight I was carrying was too heavy for me to even open up my own mouth to pray. All I could do was to listen to messages from powerful men of God and inspirational worship music to minister to my spirit. Prayers of those who loved me and knew my battle served as my strength in the time of the storm. When I finally could open my mouth to speak after a long period of just being silent, all I could do was pray. To talk about the situation was way too painful. Prayer was my saving grace. Prayer to the One who could help me was my secret comeback weapon.

> *I have gone through some things that, at the time, I thought I would never recover from.*

> *I have been in such a dark place that there was nothing left to do but to pray, pray, and pray again.*

UNSTUCK. UNLEASHED. UNSTOPPABLE.

My relief didn't come overnight. I wasn't freed instantaneously from my pain, but little by little I became stronger. One day...and I don't know when, I started to laugh again. I started to smile again. I started to recognize there was a plan for my life and the battle didn't destroy me, but proved I was a warrior.

Since my lowest point, I have still experienced days where I wanted to walk away. I still have had days that I have wanted to throw in the towel. I experienced such devastating losses and betrayals that it felt as if a Thoroughbred had repeatedly kicked me in my chest. I have gone through long seasons of suffering and had my faith in God questioned, tested, and tried. I have been in such a dark place that there was nothing left to do but to pray, pray, and pray again. Those who loved me could do nothing, but pray. The more I live, I see that not only does praying actually work, but it is always the best thing to do. In the words of Bishop Milton Hawkins, "Some things you can handle a little bit better with a prayer life." Some things you won't survive without praying because God is the only one that can work it out and after all, He is in control and really does have the final say over your life.

What do you need to stop talking about, crying about, or worrying about, and simply pray? Who can you pray for? If you can't think of anyone, what about your coworkers, employees, classmates, leaders, presidents, governors, countries, the sick, bereaved, and those around the world?

UNSTUCK. UNLEASHED. UNSTOPPABLE.

What Has Been the Hardest Lesson You Have Had to Learn?

There are no regrets in life. Just lessons.
— Jennifer Aniston

Before I was wiser, I thought there were people that I regretted befriending or dating, professions I regretted entering, and bosses I certainly regretted working with. Then, I became wiser and took another look at what I thought were my regrets. I realized they really weren't regrets, just lessons that needed to be learned. I needed to date those unworthy of my attention so that I could know what I wanted from a mate, and I could truly value and appreciate the next person. I needed to enter a profession that I hated so I could identify my purpose and passion.

I needed to enter a profession that I hated so I could identify my purpose and passion.

Take a second to look at the regrets that you think you have and change your perspective.

I needed to work for a horrible boss so I could develop character and what it means to truly honor someone who is undeserving. I needed to learn the lesson of what great leadership was and wasn't from firsthand experience. I needed to have friends betray me so I could learn what it means to guard your heart and hold your dreams sacred. I needed all of these things to happen to learn that God and my mother are the best friends that I have. No regrets, just lessons. Take a second to look at the regrets that you think you have and change your perspective. Alter the way you see that thing. What lessons have you learned through unfavorable life experiences?

What regrets do you have? What is your biggest regret? What lesson did you learn from the experience? What can you share to provide hope, healing, and encouragement to someone else?

UNSTUCK. UNLEASHED. UNSTOPPABLE.

What Are You Waiting on to Begin to Live a Life of Purpose?

You and you alone are the only person who can live the life that writes the story that you are meant to tell. And the world needs your story because the world needs your voice.
– Kerry Washington

I refuse to be held hostage by someone else's views or dreams for me. I was created for a reason and it is up to me to find out that reason. This is my story. I am the main character and within my story there will be antagonists. In my story, like so many others, you will see the main and supporting characters make great decisions and poor decisions. Sometimes the main character is a villain, and sometimes the character is a hero. It all depends on the scene that the character is in at that time. The plot will be extremely interesting and the story line will sometimes leave you on the edge of your seat. You will wonder what will happen next and just when you think you have it all figured out, there'll be another twist. Some characters in your life's story will disappear, reappear, die, plot, and scheme. Some will lie to you and others will support you. There will be epic successes and epic failures. There will be smiles and tears. Just like in any good movie, the right characters and

> *I refuse to be held hostage by someone else's views or dreams for me.*

> *Free yourself from the expectations of others and live the life that you were created to live.*

the right story line can help transform a regular actress or actor into superstardom.

Free yourself from the expectations of others and live the life that you were created to live. Live your dreams. Decide your voice will be heard about matters that are important to you. Whatever the story, remember you are the protagonist and the director, and you breathe life into the character.

I am sitting in the theater yelling at the screen, hoping you can hear me encouraging you to go after every single one of your goals. I'm pulling for you to win with what looks like a losing hand. Whatever has been written for your life, you alone can tell the story. Don't allow someone else to write the story of your life for you, because then you have given your power to someone else. Make sure your story is a story worth watching. We all love a story about a person beating the odds or overcoming adversity. I am looking for your happy ending, but you must decide. Dreams don't just come true in the movies; they come true if you write the vision and script for your life and put it in the producer's hands. Whatever you do (or don't do) affects so many others. There are people who are watching you and will go after their dreams because you had the courage to go after yours. There are people who will never reach their potential because they are patterning their life after yours consciously and subconsciously. You have impact and your life and voice matter. Someone is better or worse because of you.

 What's your story? What do you want to be written about you?

UNSTUCK. UNLEASHED. UNSTOPPABLE.

Are You Fierce and Fearless?

We live in a town that rewards pretending. I had been pretending to be fierce and fearless for a very long time. I was a victim masquerading as a survivor. I stayed when I should have run. I was quiet when I should have spoken up. I turned a blind eye to injustice instead of having the courage to stand up for what's right. I used to shrink in the presence of other dope beautiful women. I used to revel in gossip and rumors, and I lived for the negativity inflicted upon my sister actresses or anyone who I felt whose shine diminished my own. It's easy to pretend to be fierce and fearless because living your truth takes real courage. Real fearless and fierce women admit mistakes and they work to correct them. We stand up and we use our voices for things other than self-promotion. We don't stand by and let racism and sexism and homophobia run rampant on our watch. Real fearless and fierce women complement other women and we recognize and embrace that their shine in no way diminishes our light and that it actually makes our light shine brighter.
– Gabrielle Union

What's the win in commenting negatively on others? I had a former colleague who wanted me to mentor her. Although I didn't think it was a good idea for me to mentor her, I connected her with others who could assist her in helping achieve her goals. Beyond that, I engaged in other actions to assist her and took the assignment seriously.

> *The reality is there are jealous and envious people in the world who are blinded to their own greatness because of past hurts and insecurities.*

After all, I had agreed to help someone become better. There came a time when she was wearing my clothes—ones that I had given her and she stood in my face and lied, which placed me in a very uncomfortable position, compromising my character, integrity, and career. The lies she told and spread about me and my colleagues escalated to human resources. I can recall the HR professional telling me that she wasn't a person to be trusted, which was no surprise to me. What could she possibly have gained by lying about the person who was helping her?

> *To give power to a liar and someone who wasn't on my level would certainly place me on hers.*

I have never been one to think that people have been jealous of me. The reality is there are jealous and envious people in the world who are blinded to their own greatness because of past hurts and insecurities. I knew from our conversations there were demons she was running from. I just wish she could have seen her worth and her potential and realized that greatness was inside of her. It was up to her to look a little deeper and realize there is room for everyone to be successful. You don't have to dim your light or blow out someone else's for you to shine bright like the diamond you are.

My discernment had already shown me to be cordial, friendly, and professional, but to not get too close. Once the HR professional concluded telling me the mean and vicious lies this lady said about me, she asked me if I had anything to say about my mentee and I declined. She was floored and simply couldn't believe it because most people would have gladly elected to berate the person who was persecuting them. I had to explain to her that I didn't allow someone else's opinion of me to have an impact on my life. She was entitled to her viewpoint no matter how inaccurate it was.

People will always try to bring you down, but it is up to you to choose to "go high when they go low." I had nothing to gain by revealing who she really was. After all, she had already showed them her true character and that she was not of high moral character. There was nothing left for me to do. I had nothing to gain by lying about this young lady or by telling the truth and exposing her for who she truly was. She wasn't worth it in my eyes. There was no win. I wouldn't suddenly become a multi-millionaire or gain lifelong health for me and my loved ones. I wouldn't have a husband whom I respected and adored who was madly in love with me. There was no win. So to give power to a liar and someone who wasn't on my level would certainly place me on hers. Guess what? It wasn't three months later that she was gone. She couldn't take the heat of her own actions and dug her own grave.

Ask yourself, "What do I have to gain by speaking negatively of someone else?" It doesn't matter if what you are speaking is truth. What value does it add to your life to reveal things that others should learn with wisdom, discernment, and just by paying attention?

UNSTUCK. UNLEASHED. UNSTOPPABLE.

Have You Ever Thought Your Critics May Be Onto Something?

To avoid criticism—do nothing, say nothing, be nothing.
  – Elert Hubbard

Critics will always be there. They are there to let you know that you are relevant. Critics show you that you are a person worth paying attention to. Critics let you know that what you do really does matter. The sooner you can block out critics (including your overly critical viewpoint of yourself), the freer you will become. Being able to block out critics is fundamental to living freely and being yourself. People will always disagree with what you do or say. Critics are like Monday morning quarterbacks. They always provide support, insight, and unwanted feedback after the game is over. Valuable critics will help you identify the pitfalls before you mess up or make a bad decision. They are more like strategists and see things from different angles and points of view. They are not there to criticize you, but to help you become better and stronger. The only way this type of critic can serve a purpose in your life is if you listen and do something with the information being given. This critic is not sarcastically making comments and seeking to destroy your idea or your spirit. So, be wise when listening to or avoiding your critics,

> *You are not ready for extraordinary success if you cannot handle your critics.*

> *Sometimes, people will criticize us because they can see the person we are destined to become.*

UNSTUCK. UNLEASHED. UNSTOPPABLE.

for you can use what they are saying to validate and elevate yourself. You are not ready for extraordinary success if you cannot handle your critics.

For the most part, past presidents make it a point not to criticize their successors. They understand that unless you are in the role with all of the same information and advisors, you don't know what is the best decision at that time with the information you have been given. Unless you are sitting in the seat, you may not be privy to all of the information. There have been several times when I needed someone on a job to perform a role that would have made their performance so much better if I had been able to release highly confidential information. Unfortunately, I couldn't release the details to them because they weren't privy to the information at hand. People can be so critical. I remember looking at a black vehicle with leather seats and people criticized this, saying that it would be a stupid decision because Texas gets hot. Did they ever think that maybe I was cold-natured…or maybe I liked it hot?

For most of my career, I can remember always being criticized by co-workers and managers. It was as if there was a target on me for people to criticize my every move. The pressure of enduring this type of scrutiny for years can be frustrating and can make a person aloof. I had a friend whom I worked with for years, and no one ever seemed to criticize her, whereas it seemed as if I lived under a microscope. One day we were talking and she told me she just couldn't understand it because I didn't bother anyone. Over the years, other people who worked with me at various companies would witness me being criticized and would say the same thing—no one could put their hands on why I was constantly criticized unfairly. After years, I came to realize people could see the depth of my character and knew that there was more to me than what met the eye. They knew I was headed somewhere. Sometimes, people will criticize us because they can see the person we are destined to become. It's like they have a crystal ball and have walked ahead in time and cannot handle the greatness that is to come.

 Who are your critics? Are their viewpoints relevant? How can you use the information to make you better and stronger?

UNSTUCK. UNLEASHED. UNSTOPPABLE.

Are You Sacrificing Your Spirit for the Approval of Others?

It is our light, not our darkness, that most frightens us. Our deepest fear is not that we are inadequate. Our deepest fear is that we are powerful beyond measure. It is our light, not our darkness that most frightens us. We ask ourselves, who am I to be brilliant, gorgeous, talented, and fabulous? Actually, who are you not to be? You are a child of God. Your playing small does not serve the world. There's nothing enlightened about shrinking so that other people won't feel insecure around you. We were born to make manifest the glory of God that is within us. It's not just in some of us; it's in everyone. And as we let our own light shine, we unconsciously give other people permission to do the same. As we are liberated from our own fear, our presence automatically liberates others.
– Marianne Williamson

For many years, I have always had to struggle with women voicing their unsolicited opinions regarding me and who they thought I was. It got to a point where I just wanted to fly under the radar. I didn't want to bring any attention to myself. So, I would make sure that I never mentioned my level of education, certifications, neighborhood, church, or even the school that I attended. I noticed that people would begin to treat me differently if they found out what I had and then later say that I was arrogant or conceited. I would make sure that I didn't dress better or

> I will not apologize for who I am, whose I am, and what I am.

look better than any woman that I was around just to keep peace. I was dying a slow agonizing death because I couldn't be me and that's all I really wanted. I wanted to embrace the fullness of who I was without reprisal. It wasn't until later that I realized that while I was diminishing who I was for someone else to be okay with who they were, I was silently killing myself and my spirit. I was unhappy and void of signs of life. I was miserable and even with all that, I was still being treated as an outcast, as if I didn't belong.

I remember leaving a job and a female coworker gave me a card that simply said, "They hate you because they ain't you" and a pair of earrings with a star and a light. She wrote on the card that I was a star and a light. A couple of years later another female co-worker gave me a birthday card that said "B**CH"—a term for anyone who looks better, dresses better, or is smarter than you. The next year a traveling minister told me that there were lights all around me and I was meant to shine. Another traveling minister said that I needed to stop being humble and acting less than myself to make others feel better, because God wasn't happy with that. Another minister said that he could tell that I had true power and that the power made other women with perceived or manufactured power uncomfortable. Although I didn't see it, others did. I simply wanted peace and if that meant allowing others to think I was less than another, that was perfectly fine with me. I had to accept that everything works for my good and there is a reason God designed and created me this way. I am not inadequate. I am powerful. I am wonderfully and fearfully made. I will not apologize for who I am, whose I am, and what I am. If someone doesn't like it, it's too bad. They can talk to God about it because He made me, and He doesn't make mistakes.

 Who are you? Are you allowing your light to shine? Are you down-playing yourself to make others feel good about who they are? Why? How is that working for you? Embrace your beautiful self and all you were created to be.

UNSTUCK. UNLEASHED. UNSTOPPABLE.

Have You Ever Been Way in Over Your Head... Or Am I Alone?

If you aren't in over your head, how do you know how tall you are?
– T. S. Eliot

One of my most rewarding roles while working in corporate America was one that I initially thought was way too big for me. I knew that I could do the job well, but it was outside of my comfort zone and definitely not in my "sweet spot." I am an introvert and a loner, and the role required me to interact with people of various levels with different backgrounds and pretty interesting characters. I really wanted the position because I knew that I would either sink or swim. I would either stand up like a leader or sit down like an observer.

Voluntarily taking a position that I knew was over my head was frightening and intimidating, but the rewards of flourishing in that position were life-changing.

Voluntarily taking a position that I knew was over my head was frightening and intimidating, but the rewards of flourishing in that position were life-changing. The role would force me out of my comfort zone. It would challenge me in the areas in which I needed to grow and show me whether or not I was ready to move to the next level.

If you get in over your head, grab a construction helmet, put on your steel-toed boots, grab a measuring tape and some tools, go to work, and call for help.

UNSTUCK. UNLEASHED. UNSTOPPABLE.

It was the best decision I ever made. It stretched me, challenged me, and showed me that if I believed in myself and I was willing to put in the work, I could pretty much accomplish anything that I really set out to do.

I am not a person who likes to be comfortable, and I believe comfort can be an enemy to success. I love to stretch and see what I am really made of because it makes me feel stronger. I flourished in the position. I grew personally and professionally. The role tested my character, humility, influencing skills, relationship-building skills, and tolerance for blatant racism, insubordination, injustice, deceit, and so much more on a daily basis for years. I increased my grit factor, tenacity, and level of patience, while becoming even more strategic, which has always been my area of expertise.

Growing is a part of life. To whom much is given, much is required. Muster up the strength to stretch yourself in ways that you didn't think was possible. If you get in over your head, grab a construction helmet, put on your steel-toed boots, grab a measuring tape and some tools, go to work, and call for help.

When have you placed yourself in an uncomfortable position? Did you sink or swim? How did you feel? What was the end result? Remember, you are stronger and more prepared than you think.

Are You the Same Person Post-Adversity That You Are Pre-Adversity?

Adversity has a way of introducing a man to himself.
– Shia Lebeouf

During one of my most difficult and challenging seasons, I watched my childhood friend battle cancer. While it was heartbreaking to watch her fight this awful disease, it was more challenging to watch her family try to cope after she was gone. Adversity has a way of showing us what we are really made of. Are we strong and powerful? Are we optimistic? Are we a champion or a warrior? Are we a crybaby and looking for someone to join our pity party, or do we have a good cry and then go to war? Who are you?

> When the problems became more than I could handle, I found that I questioned my belief in the power of prayer and in God.

Any relationship worth its salt will be tested at some point. The essence of the relationship is determined as a result of the testing. At one point, I thought I had a pretty strong faith in God, until my faith was tested. When the problems became more than I could handle, I found that I questioned my belief in the power of prayer and in God. I found that I had moments of strength and moments of weakness. Moments when I trusted God and all His infinite power and wisdom and moments when I felt that He was allowing the enemy to just wreak havoc on my life. It felt like He had forsaken me. How could a God who loved me allow me to suffer like this for years? How long would He allow me to be depleted of energy because the intensity of the trials felt unbearable? How strong did He think I was? I understood that soldiers get wounded in battle. I understood that active soldiers may be on a tour for two, four, or six years. I wanted to be in the reserves, not active duty. Did God not understand that if I had to be deployed that I wanted a safe job? I didn't want to be on the front lines. I certainly didn't want to be unable to take a break for well over ten years. I mean this was getting ridiculous. I was being broken down like a shotgun and it appeared my God didn't even care.

How could I serve a God like that? How could I tell someone about Him when it appeared He wasn't even talking to me? Who was I? What did I really believe? Who was I becoming as a result of the continued pressure? If God never came to my rescue, what would that say about our relationship? Adversity showed me what was truly important to me and revealed to me my true character. I had much work to do. I hated the refining stage. In some ways, I was selfish. Nothing would infuriate me more than someone telling me that I wasn't experiencing life's battles for me, but for someone else. I could not care less about someone else and what they were to go through at that point; I didn't want to become stronger and certainly had no interest in anything other than my trials going away. Adversity gave me a real relationship with God. I found that I was a true believer because I got to experience Him for myself like never before. I met my God, not the God of my pastor or the God of my mother. That's when God became very real to me and I saw the scriptures come to life. God began to enter my conversations more when talking with others about their situations. My prayer life became real and I became more sensitive to the pain and needs of others. Adversity showed me that I had a heart for hurting people and to cheer for the underdog. I became more appreciative and less concerned with my own plans and more concerned with His plans for my life.

> *Adversity showed me that I had a heart for hurting people and to cheer for the underdog.*

 Who are you pre-adversity and post-adversity? What has adversity revealed to you about your character?

UNSTUCK. UNLEASHED. UNSTOPPABLE.

How Do You Climb the Mountain When You've Been in the Valley?

*Success in life comes not from holding a good hand,
but in playing a poor hand well.*
– Denis Waitley

There's something about playing Spades, especially when playing with a really good partner. I love any game of strategy. When I am able to lead or participate in strategy or brainstorming sessions, I get so excited because I am operating in one of my strongest gifts. (I feel like a good kid around Christmas time with rich parents who get me anything I want during that one time of year.) It's much easier to win with a good hand. Who can't win when they are holding all of the face cards and both jokers? It takes a pretty good player to be able to bid correctly with a poor hand and still win. One of the first persons that I met when I relocated to Texas years ago was a "First Lady" playing cards. We were paired up and had never met each other before. Yet, we are still the reigning champions, all because we were able to play the hand that we were dealt well. We would beat the cheaters and talk trash at the same time because we knew how to make the best out of the hand you've been dealt. Life is the same way.

> *I have a unique ability which allows me to quickly identify the strengths of others and put their strengths and talents to good use so we can execute efficiently and effectively.*

UNSTUCK. UNLEASHED. UNSTOPPABLE.

> *All of us can make the best out of the hand we have been dealt if we stop making excuses and start maximizing our potential.*

You have to master the hand that you are dealt because it is very rare that you will always have a winning hand. Learn how to maximize. One of my best assets and one of the things I have been warned about is building an "empire team," which can be threatening to others within an organization. That's because I believe in maximizing the strengths of myself and my team. I have a unique ability which allows me to quickly identify the strengths of others and put their strengths and talents to good use so we can execute efficiently and effectively. It's not that the weaknesses don't matter, but to win I found it's much easier to focus on what you do extremely well and outsource what you don't. I believe in leading with your strengths.

I had a friend who was a teacher and she was relocating yet again. I watched her send out resume after resume for teaching positions. I knew her writing skills were okay, but not superb. Besides, there are more applicants than positions, and she was an older teacher, which would lead some to believe her instructional practices were outdated. To some principals and HR professionals that would mean she wasn't abreast of current technology or the latest trends in education like newer teachers were, and they would have to pay her more money. During one of our conversations, I listened to her vent, and I simply told her that she had the ability to connect with others instantly and make them feel as if they had been best friends forever. I believed she had an engaging personality and if she wanted a job, she needed to knock on doors—meaning go to the school, meet with the principal, and close the deal. She needed to sell her winning personality. She did just that and has continued to do so and has never been out of a job. Ronnie, a character from the movie *The Players Club*, said "You gotta use what you got to get what you want." Most of us aren't born with a rich uncle. Most of us don't come from strong pedigree. Most of us don't know our purpose until later in life. All of us can make the best out of the hand we have been dealt if we stop making excuses and start maximizing our potential. All of us can implement the strategies necessary for success. All of us can stop entertaining ourselves and begin educating ourselves. Play the hand you've been dealt to the best of your ability and as you keep playing and studying the table. You will become better and better. One day you will win, and you will continue to win over and over again.

Use all of your experiences, history, and heritage to work for your good. How do you package everything that has happened to this point to change your life for the better?

UNSTUCK. UNLEASHED. UNSTOPPABLE.

What Are the Benefits of Knowing You?

Worry not that no one knows of you; seek to be worth knowing.
― Confucius

Who is a person worth knowing? A person worth knowing is selfless, resourceful, genuine, and authentic; has a great heart; possesses character; is life-giving instead of life-draining; and is funny, kind, impactful, insightful, and wise. A person worth knowing adds value; this person invests in others and seeks to make a difference. A person worth knowing pushes you to do more, to accomplish more, and to be more. A person worth knowing is loyal when others choose to walk away because being with you is unfavorable. A person worth knowing believes in you and holds you accountable for doing what you said, not for them, but for you. A person worth knowing loves you for you and not for what you can do for them. A person worth knowing isn't with you because they are seeking "fame by association." A person worth knowing may not have all the answers, but he or she knows how to find the right answers. A person worth knowing knows when to speak up and when to be silent…and why. A person worth knowing shows you your future instead of holding you hostage because of your past. A person worth knowing builds you up instead of tearing you down. A person worth knowing forgives your errors instead of highlighting your faults. A person worth knowing is like salt and light. They preserve you and add flavor to your life. They bring light when they come around. They are inspiring, enriching, enhancing, motivating, empowering, and uplifting.

> A person worth knowing pushes you to do more, to accomplish more, and to be more.

UNSTUCK. UNLEASHED. UNSTOPPABLE.

A person worth knowing stands up for what they believe in times of inconvenience. A person worth knowing is someone who doesn't run from adversity or conflict but who also seeks peace with all men, if possible. A person worth knowing has balance and is versatile. They can interact with presidents and powerful people, but also hold their own in the street and don't look down on people who serve them no purpose or who are "not on their level." They can impact the wise man and the foolish man with a slight turning of the wrist. A person worth knowing rises to the occasion and the strength of their character is embedded in all they do. This person is rare and that is why when you are graced with their presence, you should never take it lightly. Protect the relationship with all you've got because by observing and learning from this person's life, you will change your own. Will you have the courage to become this person?

> *A person worth knowing believes in you and holds you accountable for doing what you said, not for them, but for you.*

WARNING: *Becoming this person means you are willing to submit to a hard, lonely season as people will be attracted to you for who you are and what you bring. Many will withdraw from you instead of depositing into you. You will be misunderstood, taken for granted, persecuted, and even abandoned, but you will be a person worth knowing.*

Are you a person worth knowing? Why or why not? What makes you a person worth knowing? Who in your immediate circle is worth knowing? Have you shared it with him or her?

UNSTUCK. UNLEASHED. UNSTOPPABLE.

Do You Let Challenges Stop You from Achieving Your Goals?

The brick walls are there for a reason. The brick walls are not there to keep us out. The brick walls are there to give us a chance to show how badly we want something. Because the brick walls are there to stop the people who don't want it badly enough. They're there to stop the other people.
– Randy Pausch

The obstacle is there to serve as an evaluation tool.

How badly do you really want it? I remember talking to a gentleman about why we didn't work out. He betrayed my trust and I refused to talk to him. I would not take his calls. Years later, he told me that I put up walls to block him so that he couldn't call me, text me, or email me, but that he often thought of me and wanted to try to get back together. My response to him was that he never came for me. If he didn't have the ability to call, email, or text, he could have mailed a letter or contacted my mother or people that we both knew. In my opinion, he was making an excuse. If he really wanted to get in touch with me, he could have. I remember years earlier, when one of his sales associates told him that she wouldn't meet her goals that month because people were snowed in, he told her to get in her car and drive slow. If she knew that people were snowed in, she knew how to reach them because most of the people were at home. That same sales associate got in her car, drove slow, and exceeded the goal that month and went on to be a game changer in the industry. I believed the same principles applied here. If he really loved me and wanted me back, he would have done whatever it took to reach me. If I blocked out his phone number, I could not block out all phone numbers. If I blocked one email address, I couldn't block all available email addresses, so create a new one or go old school and mail a letter. The obstacle is there to serve as an evaluation tool.

Years later, I met another gentleman and we hit it off. As our relationship progressed, we grew fond of each other. There came a time when we felt very strongly about each other, but we knew the timing was off. He wasn't willing to make me a priority in his life as he was very focused on his other goals and nothing and no one would impede them. So, I had to make the decision that I was a priority and I loved me. I chose to walk away. I wouldn't take his phone calls and I eventually blocked him from calling me, texting me, emailing me, and on social media. I was done and I wasn't going to allow him to manipulate me with dreams of the future placing my life on hold, while he determined if there was something better out there. I believed he cared about me, but he wasn't head over heels in love with me the way he wanted me to believe. There was no reason for us to stay in contact. He would send letters or cards in the mail, call from undisclosed numbers, call me at work, or drive across town and wait for someone to leave the building, so he could sneak in the door. He would try to bribe me with good meals and offers of vacations, verbally expressing his feelings, trying to compel me with words that he wanted me. While I couldn't break because his words weren't accompanied with actions, I can appreciate that he at least displayed effort.

> *Are you willing to do whatever it takes to win?*

How badly do you really want it? Are you willing to do whatever it takes to win? If I didn't motivate him to do whatever it took to win my love again, did he really want me? And for that matter, did I really want someone who wasn't willing to go to the ends of the earth for me or at the very least, make a few phone calls or changes which challenged his ego? I know that I love deep enough that I am always willing to do whatever is necessary within the confines of the law to put a smile on the faces of those I love, so why weren't they?

Think about your deepest dreams. How badly do you want it? Do you want it badly enough to let some people go? Do you want it badly enough to make some sacrifices? If you aren't willing to make hard-core decisions and sacrifices, then you probably don't want it.

Do You Use Your Words to Create and Shape the Life You Want?

What you have is a direct result of what you are saying or not saying.
– Unknown

For years, I would focus on watching my words and do my very best to not speak negatively. I tried to make sure that my words did not result in the death of my dreams or would serve to usher in anything that I did not want in my life. While it is definitely necessary to not speak negatively, it's just as important to speak positive words over your life. That's where I was coming up short. I had been so disappointed in my life that I just didn't speak positively or negatively anymore. I had allowed life to beat me up and defeat me. It would take the words of a powerful woman to shed light that I didn't have a lot of the things I wanted because I failed to open up my mouth and speak what I wanted. I am so grateful that she called me out on my shortcomings.

> *Your words are like seeds that you are planting today for a harvest tomorrow.*

Words have power. Your words are like seeds that you are planting today for a harvest tomorrow. If you want a better future, begin cultivating your future by speaking words of encouragement, inspiration, motivation, empowerment, and faith. Say out loud what you desire as if it has already happened. Don't just

> *Use your words to bring your dreams to life.*

speak the words, but speak the words with power. Speak the words as if your very life depended on it. When life seems unbearable, it is then that you must dig deep within and watch your words and speak life into your own life. I'm sure you have heard people say that they didn't think that things could get worse. You talk to them a couple of days or months later and things are worse. They put it out in the atmosphere. Stop saying everything you feel, and use your words as one of your secret weapons to change things.

What if we only received what we spoke? Would you speak more? It's not enough to think it—you have got to see it. You can never see it, if you are unable to speak it. Open your mouth and speak what you want into the atmosphere. Use your words to bring your dreams to life.

How do you use your words as a secret weapon to unleash victories, promises, dreams, and accomplishments? Speak what you want for yourself, your family, future generations, your communities, presidents, countries, and the world. I dare you to open your mouth and speak daily the very thing that you desire to see take place.

UNSTUCK. UNLEASHED. UNSTOPPABLE.

How Competitive Are You?

I play to win, whether during practice or a real game. And I will not let anything get in the way of me and my competitive enthusiasm to win.
— Michael Jordan

Whatever I do, I want to win. Winning is who I am and what I do. I don't care if I am playing a friendly game of Spades or the game of life. I will always do my best. I remember bowling for the first time with my former leader and mentor. I had not bowled in years, and I have never been a good bowler, but I am a very competitive person. When we entered the bowling alley, I immediately began to talk so much trash that we had the time of our life. I gave it my very best. We still laugh to this day because he swears that is the day I truly opened up, let go, and he saw me in a completely different light. One day we were talking and I asked him if he thought I was competitive and he gave me a resounding, "Yes."

> *Develop a will to win regarding your business, family, marriage, career, job, and relationships.*

> *If you really want to win, you'll give it all you've got because you know that the taste of victory is ever so sweet.*

One of my coworkers used to say that she didn't care who held the trophy, but she just wanted to win. My response was that I wanted to win and hold the trophy because I was the MVP and the owner and that's what we do. The trophy is given to us first and we share it with the rest of the team, because we led the team to victory while making a major contribution. People often ask if I am competitive and I am.

Although I'm not in competition with anyone else, I compete with me (who I was yesterday and last year) and who I know I can become, if I focus my energy on becoming the best version of myself. I play to win. Anyone who says that winning doesn't matter probably hasn't won enough, because winning can become addicting.

Develop a will to win regarding your business, family, marriage, career, job, and relationships. A will to win is a competitive edge that everyone doesn't have and can help propel you to victory in every area of your life. The desire to win is contagious and can help catapult others who are around you to do better in their lives as well. If you really want to win, you'll give it all you've got because you know that the taste of victory is ever so sweet.

What do you need to do to step up your game to win? Ask yourself, "Do I want to win?"

UNSTUCK. UNLEASHED. UNSTOPPABLE.

Are You Governed by How You Feel?

Successful people do what they have to do, whether they feel like it or not.
– Unknown

Selfish. Narcissist. It's all about you. Everything is not all about you. Those are the words often ringing in my ear because I have made a concrete choice to be successful and that choice requires, no it demands, sacrifices. There are things I can't do because I have made up my mind to achieve my goals. I know what it means to have to turn down a date with a potential suitor who appeared to be extremely successful and into me because I needed to work on achieving my goals that day. I had to stay the course and remain focused. He was currently in a place that I desired to be,

> Get used to making sacrifices if you want to be successful.

and I'm sure at one point he had to be selfish with his time as well. So, although I wanted to go out, I couldn't. I needed to read. Some may think reading a book is nothing and that I really didn't like that person, but that is the furthest thing from the truth. The truth is, I did like him. Successful people engage daily in personal development. I didn't want to read every day, but I wanted to grow. I did not want to move to Austin, Texas, but I wanted to transition from teaching to corporate America. I didn't want to drive my same car for years, but I wanted investments, money in the bank, and an opportunity to travel the world. I didn't want to work out and limit my carb intake, but I didn't want to gain weight. I didn't want to distance myself from certain people, but I wanted to become more positive. I didn't want to say that I couldn't go to the movies when I really did, but I needed to work on my business goals.

It is a series of small, daily commitments that separates the successful from the unsuccessful. It's our choices that make a difference. One day, living the life that you desire requires you to do now what you have to do, so that later you can do what you want to do. What do you need to do now to be successful later? There are plenty of things I don't want to do, but one thing I know for sure is that successful people do what they have to do…whether they like it or not. Because they are willing to make the sacrifices, they should reap the reward. What are you willing to change up now to be successful later? Sometimes, you must be a little selfish and sacrificing to be successful. It's not always pretty, but often worth it. Get used to making sacrifices if you want to be successful. If you want to be comfortable and not see many of your dreams come true, continue on with life as usual.

You cannot be governed by your emotions if you want to be successful. Things won't always feel good. What are you willing to do to participate in your own success?

UNSTUCK. UNLEASHED. UNSTOPPABLE.

What's Your Grit Factor?

You must knock on doors until your knuckles bleed. Doors will slam in your face. You must pick yourself up, dust yourself off, and knock again. It's the only way to achieve your goals in life.
– Michael Ulsan

Looking for a job can be one of the most challenging experiences that one can go through. The constant rejection can be brutal to your ego and can really mess with your psyche. You apply for job after job, ones for which you are more than qualified, and you hear nothing. You apply and you get the letter that said they selected another candidate. You apply and receive an interview. Celebrate! You move to phase two, phase three. You wait. You hear nothing. Rejection. Now, the process starts all over again.

> *You've got to develop mental toughness and grit if you want to achieve your goals.*

Now, you are in the battlefield of your mind. You are in the fight for your life. This is what so many people must go through.

No one likes rejection, but we all must face it. So what do you do? If you are like me, you find a way to keep your sanity. I am not a quitter. I am determined to win and I love a challenge. So, here we go. Who wants to play the game of a hundred NOs? How long will it take me to reach one hundred NOs? To get to one hundred NOs requires me to be resilient (to shake the dust off) and try again because it's the only way I can achieve my goals. As long as I am getting a no, I am one step closer to achieving my goals because there will be some yeses along the way. You've got to develop mental toughness and grit if you want to achieve your goals.

 What do you want? Sometimes, perseverance is key. Keep knocking and knocking until you get what you want.

What Excuses Are You Making Because You Failed to Execute Properly?

You can make excuses or you can make money, but you can't do both.
— Otis Broadwater

Some people call them excuses and others call them reasons. Whatever your term of preference, the fact remains that you failed to do what you said you would and in most cases, that is simply unacceptable. Things come up unexpectedly and that is part of life, but for a successful person, it's simply not the norm. Not accomplishing your goal as a person of success is the exception to the rule. You either did it or you didn't, and oftentimes the reason or excuse doesn't matter.

When you miss the mark and fail to achieve your goal, what's next on the agenda? Do you quit or do you go out there and work extra hard to make up for what you didn't do? Do you plan better next time? Do you own the fact that you came up short? Do you re-strategize? We have all heard it said that excuses are tools of incompetence used to build monuments of nothingness, and those who specialize in them seldom accomplish anything.

> *Things come up unexpectedly and that is part of life, but for a successful person, it's simply not the norm.*

On my team, I rarely ask someone what happened if they drop the ball. That is because I set the expectation that we will execute on time and on or under budget, and we will communicate the risks up front so there are no surprises. Unless something is major, I don't discuss why something didn't happen because I just want it fixed now. The bottom line is that it didn't happen and I hate excuses. Let's fix the problem, discuss what worked well, what didn't, and what we need to do differently. The same is held true in my personal life. I either did it or I didn't, and I would rather plan and execute than discuss excuses or reasons why I fell short.

 What excuses are you making? There will always be a reason why you can't do something, but there will also be a reason why you can. Stop making excuses and just get it done.

UNSTUCK. UNLEASHED. UNSTOPPABLE.

Are You Aware of the Number of People Who Are Watching You?

Every closed eye is not sleeping, and every open eye is not seeing.
– Bill Cosby

> *Work on your character before you are elevated.*

There are people who act like they are not listening to a conversation, but they are there, taking it all in. They may never say a word regarding the conversation at hand, but they can give you a complete play-by-play of everything that was said, including the facial expressions. Be cognizant of what you are saying and doing and the image you present. Make sure your character matches your calling. Work on your character before you are elevated.

People are watching you and paying attention to you. Some are even studying your every move. It has been interesting to see on Facebook that I can post something, and there are people who are observing and spectating. They will never like an image or share a post. I would never know that they had seen anything until I talk to them and they give me a rundown of what's been happening in my life.

> *Just because two people are looking at the same thing does not mean they are seeing the same thing.*

Just because two people are looking at the same thing does not mean they are seeing the same thing. Both view through a lens based upon their experiences, cultures, histories, upbringing, and so forth, which shapes his or her unique perspective. So, it's shallow to judge someone based upon your vision and their viewpoint.

 Is there someone that you admire from afar? What have you observed about their character?

UNSTUCK. UNLEASHED. UNSTOPPABLE.

Do You Often Feel Misunderstood When Sharing Your Dreams?

You cannot explain to a turtle a giraffe decision.
– Bishop T. D. Jakes

This is major. Giraffes have a different perspective of life from their viewpoint than a turtle has from his. Giraffes see up high and turtles are down low. Think about it like this: When you are flying in an airplane, you are able to see the world, even your city, from a different viewpoint in the air than you can when you are driving around on the ground. It is a waste of your time and mental energy to try and explain to someone who cannot see from your perspective, why you made a certain choice.

> *It is a waste of your time and mental energy to try and explain to someone who cannot see from your perspective, why you made a certain choice.*

Our perspectives differ and I owe it to no one to explain my decision, especially if it doesn't impact him or her. Visionaries, those blessed with creativity, eccentric and/or quirky people, dreamers, those who think outside of the box (or who, better yet, desire to own the box) may often be misunderstood, especially by those with limited vision. The more you surround yourself with those who differ from you, the more exposure you receive, the broader your thinking becomes. The broader,

> *Where they saw a challenge, I saw opportunity.*

your thinking, the more you stand a chance of not fitting in. When you don't fit in, people don't understand you, and when they can't understand you, guess what? They criticize you. I've had those who loved me and cared for me challenge the validity of the decisions I've made. Where they saw a challenge, I saw opportunity.

The most successful person I know once said that whenever he has a major decision or is making a major move, he never shares it with anyone because he doesn't want to have to explain his choice to the naysayers and those who don't have his dreams and vision. When it's the right timing and the door opens, you have to walk through, no matter how crazy it may look or sound to others. They won't understand it in the beginning, so explaining it at this point serves no purpose. Some people have to see it to believe it. My view of Paris during the day was completely different once I saw it in the evening. Everything looks better in the light. Different views yield different perspectives. Quit trying to explain your decisions to those who have vision, but cannot see. You'll only be frustrated and possibly discouraged.

 Why do you feel the need to have others validate your ideas or decisions? If you need to share, are you sharing with the right people?

UNSTUCK. UNLEASHED. UNSTOPPABLE.

Do You Allow the Actions of Others to Extinguish Your Flame?

Man's goodness is a flame that can be hidden but never extinguished.
– Nelson Mandela

My mother would always say that it's just nice to be nice. I have found that goodness has a way of having a trickle-down effect and leaves a legacy for years to come. My mother is probably the kindest person I know. For years, I have watched her help and take care of others who were overlooked by others. I have seen her be selfless and be the voice for those who had no voice. Her genuine loving-kindness flows through my veins and is one of the things I sometimes wish I could change about myself. I sometimes want to treat others the way they treat me, but I can't. Sometimes, I want to return evil for evil, but I can't. I just sit and cry and pick myself back up, vowing to not be so soft-hearted in the future. The future comes and I remember my mother's words, "It's just nice to be nice." And there I go again—being nice.

> *I have found that goodness has a way of having a trickle-down effect and leaves a legacy for years to come.*

> *It just makes sense that you would be nice to someone who is nice to you, but what about those who treat you unkindly?*

UNSTUCK. UNLEASHED. UNSTOPPABLE.

It just makes sense that you would be nice to someone who is nice to you, but what about those who treat you unkindly? I like to say that how you treat me can't stop me from going to heaven, but how I treat you will. One of the things that I absolutely adore is to make those I love laugh and smile. It warms my heart. I have found that volunteering for worthy causes and participating in random acts of kindness are a great way for me to spread joy and share kindness to others. Although you shouldn't show goodness to others because of what you will receive, the reality is that goodness has a way of following and catching up to you. You sow seeds of goodness, and you reap love, joy, fulfillment, satisfaction, grace, and mercy. Doing good is a light from within that shines outwardly and reaches so many.

Will you help start a goodness revolution and leave a lasting legacy of kindness for future generations? We need it now more than ever. When was the last time you did good for someone that you weren't required to? How can you show goodness today? Make it a habit to show goodness to a stranger at least once per week.

UNSTUCK. UNLEASHED. UNSTOPPABLE.

Do You Fight Back and Win?

He has the heart of a lion and the spirit of a warrior.
– Wayne Drash

> *It takes courage and strength to stand in the face of adversity, to have hope against all hope.*

This quote was referenced to someone who went to school with me. Desmond Merriweather was battling terminal cancer yet still giving his all to make a difference in the Memphis community, even seeking the assistance of a childhood friend from his neighborhood (former NBA player Anfernee "Penny" Hardaway) to take over his coaching responsibilities, when he was too sick to continue to lead the team. While facing a death sentence, he continued to show up for practice after undergoing chemo, to be there for his "kids." A lot of us would be at home whining or giving in to our emotions. Some of us would be focused on our own families. Instead, Desmond was working hard on his deathbed to make sure his "kids" (players) were taken care of, and he had left someone to be a role model to them.

What kind of toll does the weight of continued sickness do to one's spirit? Desmond continued to fight to live for his students and provide them with a role model of worthy character. It takes courage and strength to stand in the face of adversity, to have hope against all hope. Being a warrior requires discipline and training to win. You must be fit for the battle to be a

> *It takes an incredible amount of courage to give it one more fight when there is no fight left in you.*

warrior. Training to become a warrior is how you respond to small battles. Do you quit? Do you give up when things don't go your way? Do you cower down when you should stand up? Everyone isn't fit to be a warrior because some people don't want to discipline themselves enough to have a lifestyle of victory. Some people don't want to exercise bravery because it may require them to lose some things. Some people are just too weak for battle because they haven't developed their propensity to win. They never go through anything because they can't handle anything.

It takes an incredible amount of courage to give it one more fight when there is no fight left in you. Courage to smile when you feel like crying. Courage to show vulnerability when your head is saying otherwise. Courage to go on another day when there is no obvious win or peace in sight. I am a proud Central Warrior. Warriors fight back and win. A warrior is prepared to battle and will experience battle after battle and win. Fighting continuously can take its toll on you and break you down. It can zap your strength if you are not fit for battle. It takes skill as well as courage to be a warrior. You have to know how to fight to win and not become distracted by the people who are watching to see if you can fight back and win.

You may win the battle, but I will win the war. I have trained for this. I have endured and persevered. I have heart and tenacity and can look fear in the face and still pursue the enemy no matter who or what it is…including me, even if I am the enemy to myself, if necessary. Determination and dedication undergirded by truth, wisdom, and strategy, are all a part of my battle plan. I cannot and will not be defeated. If you're waiting to see my demise, I suggest you plan your funeral because you'll die waiting. You will never see it as long as I have breath in my body. I live to fight another day. I was built to win! Anything worth having is worth fighting for. Your dreams are worth you giving it all you've got. Your future is worth you getting up and giving it another shot. You are worth having the courage it takes to maximize your potential and not giving in or giving up. Get back in the ring because I'm not throwing in the towel or calling the match. Fight back and win!

 What are you willing to fight for? Are your beliefs, values, dreams, and family worth you giving it all you've got? Is it worth facing the fear and doing it anyway (whatever your "it" is)?

Have You Ever Made a Decision That You Later Regretted?

*You're panicking, Sonny,
and I intend to take full advantage of that.*
– Quote from the movie Draft Day

Never make a decision based upon your emotions, because there's a pretty good chance it will be one that you may regret. So many people voluntarily place themselves in horrible situations because they panicked. They didn't take time to really think through the decision they were facing and search for the best solution given the problem at hand. When you are in a desperate situation, I would strongly suggest that you take a time out. Walk away from the situation and just breathe. If you have a trusted advisor who is great at looking at things from different angles, it may be helpful to talk through the problem at hand with them. A fresh perspective, another set of eyes, and a good night's rest may be just what the doctor ordered to keep you from making a rash decision that could cost you dearly later.

When you panic, there are vultures out there who will not hesitate to use your weakness for their advantage. Predators are out there lurking…looking for poor and innocent people who can support their agenda. The housing market is a good example of this. Let's take a look: There is someone who has waited for years before purchasing their dream home. The time finally comes when they are ready to make the purchase. They get approved for the loan and are set to close. Closing day arrives and they are excited. They go to closing and the numbers are all wrong. The monthly mortgage is more than they thought. What do they do? They have told everyone about their new purchase. What will people think? The movers are set to come the next day. They have to be out of their current home because they have rented it out, so where will they go? The new payment is more than they can easily handle. If they move forward with the deal, nothing can happen with their finances or they will bust. There are countless stories like this. Unfortunately, some people will move forward with the deal anyway.

> *A fresh perspective, another set of eyes, and a good night's rest may be just what the doctor ordered to keep you from making a rash decision that can cost you dearly later.*

I actually received a call from someone who was in a similar situation to this one. The person asked my opinion. I advised her to walk away, and let the title company and realtors work it out. She was scared. I assured her that they definitely wanted to close the deal. Someone involved in the transaction had a lot riding on the closing and would influence the others to make the deal work. Guess what? Everything worked out to her advantage, without her having to bear the financial responsibility. A lot of people would have panicked and signed the papers and found themselves deep in debt with a payment they couldn't handle, possibly facing foreclosure later on or bad credit due to being neglectful with their other debts.

When you make decisions based upon your emotions, expect to falter and worse…to be taken advantage of. When someone tries to pressure me to make a decision at that very moment, they have just made the decision for me—and that decision is to walk away with no regrets. If it is not a life and death situation, what's the hurry?

What are some decisions that you are currently facing? Are you making the decision with a clear head? Do you have any doubt at all that you will regret your decision later? If you don't have full peace with your decision, then why don't you just wait a little while.

UNSTUCK. UNLEASHED. UNSTOPPABLE.

Whose Opinion is More Valued? Your Own or the Naysayers?

You have given me a thousand reasons why something won't work; now just give me one reason why it will.
– Unknown

It won't work. We've tried it before. If we do it that way, then…We can't, because… UGH! Somebody come and save me from all of the pessimists in the world! While it's great to share with me all of the reasons why something won't work, let's expend energy on the one reason why something will. What if the one reason actually worked? Yes, things can go wrong and sometimes they have been tried before, but people and times change. Maybe the universe was simply not ready for what you were offering at that time.

> *Instead of her encouraging me or offering to help, she asked me, "What makes you think that hasn't been done before?"*

I can recall working on developing an idea that I thought was pretty solid. As a matter of fact, I thought it was MAJOR! I shared my idea with someone who I thought would be supportive. Instead of her encouraging me or offering to help, she asked me, "What makes you think that hasn't been done before?" She then said, "We actually tried it and it was a failure." She proceeded to give me all of the reasons she could think of to prove to me that I was not on the right track. When I asked her to help me identify why the idea *would* work, she was speechless. I had a number of reasons why it would work, including the timing couldn't have been better for the product.

UNSTUCK. UNLEASHED. UNSTOPPABLE.

Don't allow anyone to dismiss your idea because they believe it can't be done.

When we look at President Obama and even Democratic presidential nominee Hillary Clinton, they both are proof that just because something hasn't worked previously, it doesn't mean that it won't work now. Hillary Clinton made her first run for office in 2008 and wasn't elected. It wasn't her time. Instead, President Obama was the first African-American presidential nominee for either party and went on to be elected the first African-American president. There have been African-Americans who have run for president before, and none were elected until the time was right. Many people thought America would never elect an African-American president. However, we did and we made history.

You may have an idea…whether for your business, career, family, church, community, or otherwise. Don't allow anyone to dismiss your idea because they believe it can't be done. That's their perspective, and they are entitled to think that way. You may need to improve your selling or influencing skills by presenting your ideas in a different way. You also could implement a brainstorming session to help people talk through why your idea could work. Another suggestion is to host a think tank to generate ideas of how to make to it work. It's very possible that your idea will work if you work it. A focus group will allow you to validate your concept.

What ideas have you tossed aside because you allowed someone else's opinion to dissuade you from moving forward? What ideas could work if you repositioned how you presented your idea to others?

UNSTUCK. UNLEASHED. UNSTOPPABLE.

Do You Have What It Takes to Win Against Someone Just as Stronger, if Not Stronger, Than Yourself?

You have to defeat a great player's aura more than his game.
– Pat Riley

Winning first starts in your head. What do you think of your opponent? Are they better than you, stronger than you, more prepared than you, been in the game longer than you? It's mental. Whatever you think, you will manifest. As a man thinketh, so is he. To defeat a player, you have to be able to get in their head, their mind, and take them to a place where they don't want to go. Win the game *before* you win the game.

> *Winning first starts in your head.*

There have been times when I knew that someone who doesn't know me has decided for whatever reason that they just didn't like me. I have had women try and stare me down, ignore me when I enter a room, talk negatively about me loud enough that I can hear them, and use several other tactics to try to intimidate me. I laugh, I smile, and I go on with my activity as if nothing happened. You see, I understand that they are trying to get into my head and defeat my aura. They want to put enough pressure on me to make me break—to prove that I am just like them or not as I portray myself.

> *Win the game before you win the game.*

UNSTUCK. UNLEASHED. UNSTOPPABLE.

The beauty is I use it as a tool to ignite a fire inside of me to step my game up, not let them see me sweat, to hustle even harder. When you don't let them see you sweat, it messes with their aura. They can't understand why you are not shaken or moved because they would be. If they only knew how they are actually helping me, propelling me forward, they wouldn't do it. It becomes a driving force. It's not easy to defeat a great player's game because they put a lot of effort, time, and practice into developing their skill. They work on their skills continuously to become great. Before major presentations, I do my best to "get my head right." It's vital so I can deliver successfully. I don't want to focus on what's wrong or the negative energy that some people may bring, and that's the same with a great player.

If you can get into that small space of defeating a person's aura, you can throw his game off. It takes a lot of strength to not display emotion in front of your opponent, but it's well worth it. There have been times when I have been able to totally throw my opponent off their game, to the point of no recovery, simply by not letting them know that they were getting to me. I have found by acting as if your opponent is so far removed from your level to be one of the best strategies at defeating them mentally. This strategy is very effective when you combine it with studying your opponent. When you can mentally disarm your opponent, you have pretty much won the battle. All you need to do at that point is to increase the pressure and execute your strategy.

If the opponent can impact your aura more than your game, they have the secret and will use it every time. All winners have opponents—people who desire to see us fail (overtly and covertly).

What can you do to sweeten your game with your opponent?

UNSTUCK. UNLEASHED. UNSTOPPABLE.

How Resourceful Are You?

You can throw me butt-naked in the jungle and I'll come out with a chinchilla coat, a leopard hat, and ten pounds heavier.
– Sean Combs

Intelligent. Focused. Driven. Sean P. Diddy Combs is a force to be reckoned with. He is certainly a person hungry for success and is willing to do what it takes to thrive. Sometimes, the opportunity itself isn't as important as what you do with the opportunity that's presented. Working harder than others, staying focused, seeing your dreams in color, and then making those same dreams into a box-office hit takes grit. It means not seeing obstacles, but seeing solutions, victories, and accomplishments. You've got to see the end in the very beginning. You've got to believe in yourself. If you truly believe in yourself, then you've got to run toward your dreams. Invest in yourself first before you ask anyone else to invest in you. You've got to make things happen. Make the most out of what you have right now, because if you stay the course, you will attain the success you are striving for. It won't always be like this. Where you are right now is temporary if you will think like Diddy and determine that nothing can hold you back from your success.

> Sometimes, the opportunity itself isn't as important as what you do with the opportunity that's presented.

> You've got to believe in your God-given gifts, talents, and abilities and dare to take a chance on yourself.

I know it can be scary to stand on the edge of the ledge and dare to jump! You've got to believe in your God-given gifts, talents, and abilities and dare to take a chance on yourself. If you have vision and are certain of the purpose of your life, then jump. Stop being fearful.

UNSTUCK. UNLEASHED. UNSTOPPABLE.

Stop making excuses. Stop procrastinating. Dare to be different and jump. What do you have to lose? The only way you can fail is if you don't try and you don't learn.

 You can either die in the jungle or make the jungle an empire. What do you want for yourself?

UNSTUCK. UNLEASHED. UNSTOPPABLE.

Bitter or Better?

If you continuously compete with others, you become bitter, but if you continuously compete with yourself, you become better.
– Unknown

Records are meant to be broken. There will always be someone that looks better than you, has a better body, a more pleasing personality, is better connected than you, is more intelligent…but there's only one you. There will be someone who speaks better, dresses better, and is better educated. If you compare yourself to others and what they have acquired, achieved, or accomplished, you will always be in a competition that you just can't win. You can't maintain and sustain your mental and emotional energy successfully by focusing on others, when you take your eyes off what's important, and that's you and your goals.

> *If you compare yourself to others and what they have acquired, achieved, or accomplished, you will always be in a competition that you just can't win.*

From now on, you are in a competition with you (and you only!), and that is to be the best version of you that you can be. Your goal is to live successfully and authentically. Your prize is your liberty, your freedom, your joy. At this point, your focus is to maximize your potential and to die with no regrets. Who really wants to die with unused potential? What can you accomplish if you lived life on purpose by fully optimizing your gifts, talents, and abilities?

As I compete with who I was yesterday, the me of today wins. Today, I have another opportunity to become better. Today, I will learn. Today, I will grow. Today, I will forgive. Today, I will be brave. Today, I will be great. Tomorrow, I will be better. Tomorrow, I will be wiser. Tomorrow, I will be stronger.

 What skills do you need to sharpen to become a better version of yourself? How are you better today than you were yesterday?

UNSTUCK. UNLEASHED. UNSTOPPABLE.

How Committed Are You to the Things that Really Matter to You?

If you aren't going all the way, why go at all?
– Joe Namath

Give it all you've got. How badly do you want it? Why play if you aren't playing to win? I am extremely competitive. I love to win. I expect to win. I don't understand why you would do anything worthwhile if you are not going to give it your best shot. If I decide to be a friend, I am the best friend you can possibly have. I try to be the best daughter I can be. If I am at work, I expect to complete projects on time and under budget with minimal negative impact. I expect to win the performance awards, to get the best raises. I expect my business to be successful because I'm going to give it all I've got. I'm going to fully commit to the process.

> I don't understand why you would do anything worthwhile if you are not going to give it your best shot.

I am amazed at people who expect great outcomes but want to put forth little to no effort. You want to win, but are you willing to give it your all? Give your goals your best shot. What would happen or what could happen if you decided to put it all on the line? Why get married if you aren't going to give it your all? If you're still going to live like you are single, then why would you make a lifelong commitment to one person? If you're going to start your own business, then why not put more effort into working for yourself than you do working for someone else? If you are going to work a job, why not do everything you can to maximize your earning potential? Why would you become a parent if you are not going to be the best mother or father possible, doing everything you can to fully prepare your child to succeed when they are out on their own? Why compete on the team if you aren't going to fully commit?

What would happen or what could happen if you decided to put it all on the line?

If you're not going to give it your all, stop putting yourself into situations where you aren't willing to do what it takes to thrive. When you don't fully commit to yourself, subconsciously you are letting yourself down. When you make it a habit of letting yourself down, you eventually find you are questioning your capabilities and doubting what you really are capable of. While it's important that you give the things that really matter your all, it is also important to know when perfection is your enemy. So, while you are giving your all to the things that are important, be careful that you don't allow perfection to impede your progress when it really isn't necessary.

What areas of your life do you need to recommit yourself to and be "all in?" What has been the result of not fully committing yourself to the areas that really matter to you?

UNSTUCK. UNLEASHED. UNSTOPPABLE.

Do You Learn from Your Defeats?

I will not lose, for even in defeat, there's a valuable lesson learned so that evens it up for me.
— Jay Z

> The most valuable lessons I have learned have been the lessons learned when the end result did not turn out favorably.

Okay, so by now you know that I love to win. However, there are times when I am not as successful as I want to be. The most valuable lessons I have learned have been the lessons learned when the end result did not turn out favorably. On the outside looking in, it appeared that I had lost, but in actuality, I won. I won because I learned the lesson. Because of a failed relationship, I learned how to choose better partners. I learned how to look at a person's actions instead of listening to their words. I learned how to believe what people show me the first time instead of hoping that they will change. I learned what it's like to truly love unconditionally. Because I had to taste defeat, I trained harder and learned the importance of conditioning, because I never wanted to experience defeat again. I learned to decide ahead of time what I really wanted and to not underestimate what it would take to achieve whatever it is I wanted.

I was talking with a former co-worker. She was working way too many hours under a new boss. She had no work-life balance.

> Because I had to taste defeat, I trained harder and learned the importance of conditioning, because I never wanted to experience defeat again.

> *Quit pressing the rewind button, replaying your past indiscretions and failures over and over.*

Many people would often tell her that she needed to slow down. She wouldn't listen. She ended up getting laid off due to a restructuring. On her last day at the company where she had worked for well over twenty years, she went to the emergency room and was immediately admitted to the hospital, where she remained in ICU for six days. The doctors informed her she had diabetes and her sugar was so high they couldn't register it. She had no family or medical history of diabetes. The doctors attributed the diabetes to stress. They placed her on two daily doses of insulin, along with other medicines. Two months later, she was off her medicines. The layoff may have saved her life. Now, she practices work-life balance.

Okay, so you may have messed up. You may have not given your very best this time. You may have given it your all, and your all just wasn't good enough. That's okay, because it happens to the best of us. No one is up all the time. Stop replaying the perceived failure over and over in your mind. Quit pressing the rewind button, replaying your past indiscretions and failures over and over. Sometimes, you may take a test and get an A. Other times, you may take a test and the grade is a D. You barely passed, but the point is that you passed. You passed not because you got just enough right, but because you had enough common sense to learn something from the experience. Maybe, just maybe, the defeat was there disguised as a win so you could learn the most valuable lesson.

What defeat did you take the hardest? What did you learn from it? Because if you didn't learn anything, then yes, you really did lose.

UNSTUCK. UNLEASHED. UNSTOPPABLE.

What's the Difference Between Temporary Defeat and Failure?

There is a difference between temporary defeat and failure.
– Napoleon Hill

There is a huge difference between temporary defeat and failure. Failure is a mind-set. It is a deep-rooted belief that on a consistent basis, you don't achieve your goals. Temporary defeat is understanding that this one goal wasn't attainable for you this time. It is knowing beyond a shadow of a doubt "it" got you this time, but it didn't get the best of you. When you understand that you are temporarily defeated, you can immediately come to the conclusion that you will recover and be better than ever.

> *There is a huge difference between temporary defeat and failure.*

Distinguishing between temporary defeat and failure requires an evaluation of your thinking. Just because you missed the mark in this one endeavor, in no way, shape, or form does it mean you are a failure at everything. It simply means you are human and sometimes you won't knock the ball out of the ballpark. Guess what? You learn from the temporary defeat. You regroup. You tweak your strategy, study your opponent, and refine your game plan.

> *Just because you missed the mark in this one endeavor, in no way, shape, or form does it mean you are a failure at everything.*

 What temporary defeat was so life-changing that it rocked your perception of who you are and made you think you were a failure? I don't care how long you have been in a state of temporary defeat. Decide today that you are never a failure. Now, let's go get it.

UNSTUCK. UNLEASHED. UNSTOPPABLE.

What Does Pressure Do to You and for You?

Pressure produces cupcakes or diamonds.
– Antonio Adair

> Pressure produces champions, but it can also make the strongest of people crumble.

There is nothing like pressure to show you who you are and what you are made of. Pressure can crush you like a cupcake or refine you like a diamond. Pressure produces champions, but it can also make the strongest of people crumble. Pressure will pull out what is inside of you. Prolonged pressure has a way of making you bitter or better, but you have to decide how you will handle the pressure.

I remember working at a company, and the pressure there appeared to be insurmountable. I was under a tremendous amount of pressure, and my colleagues were looking for me to break. They thought the pressure would break me. Little did they know, I truly believed that I had the "heart of a warrior and the spirit of a champion." My high school mascot was a warrior. I had already been predestined to handle pressure long before this incident. They would never see me crumble like a cupcake. I had dealt with so much pressure in my life by that point that, although it was hard, I could overcome. Now, I am not saying that I didn't have bad days and long nights, but I knew that the pressure was to make a better Sharalyn and not to break Sharalyn. So, game on.

> The pressure showed me how mentally tough I was, the areas that I needed to develop, and my level of commitment to achieving my goals.

UNSTUCK. UNLEASHED. UNSTOPPABLE.

The pressure showed me how mentally tough I was, the areas in which I needed to develop, and my level of commitment to achieving my goals. I chose not to crumble under the pressure but to hold my head high in my enemies' presence. I chose to smile and learn the lesson needed to become an invaluable jewel—a value-added resource. Pressure produces diamonds and diamonds are rare. Don't allow the pressure to take over. Don't allow it to break you. Find something that brings you joy—even temporary relief (as long as it's not illegal or addicting)—and allow that to be your outlet. It can be something as simple as a walk in the park, a dance in the rain, or a movie night with your favorite person. Just do whatever it takes to not crumble under the pressure.

What is pressure turning you into—a cupcake or a diamond? Have you made up in your mind that the pressure will not break you? What is the pressure producing inside of you?

UNSTUCK. UNLEASHED. UNSTOPPABLE.

What Do You Want More Than Success?

When you want to succeed as much as you want to breathe, that's when you will be successful.
– Les Brown and Eric Thomas

I love this quote. It really boils down to a matter of will. How badly do you want it? There is no other option for me but to be successful. I eat, sleep, and breathe, striving for success. It is part of my DNA. I believe that if I was cut open today, you would see the word "success" written all over my organs. It is a part of me. I need to succeed just as much as I need air, food, and water. I surround myself with successful people. The television shows I watch are shows of strategy and business that develop me in one way or another. I feed my mind with the images of the things I want to accomplish—whatever that may be. I place success in the forefront of my mind, and I work daily to make the dreams and visions I have for my life come alive. I don't let anyone tell me that I can't be successful. When I'm feeling down, I get up and watch, read, or listen to something that will revitalize my spirit. By guarding what I take in my eye and ear gates, I am better able to battle the things that can discourage or distract me and cause me to lose focus.

> *I place success in the forefront of my mind, and I work daily to make the dreams and visions I have for my life come alive.*

> *The very thought of leaving this earth, unsuccessful with unused talent, is frightening and can very easily send me into a state of depression.*

UNSTUCK. UNLEASHED. UNSTOPPABLE.

I used to hear that your "why" should make you cry. I never had anything that I would say was so important to me that the thought of not obtaining it would bring me to tears. When I really became certain that I wanted success in every area of my life, that I wanted to create a life that I was absolutely in love with and help others to do the same, is when I got it. The very thought of leaving this earth, unsuccessful with unused talent, is frightening and can very easily send me into a state of depression. The idea of being unsuccessful is unbearable.

Ask yourself, "How badly do I want to be successful?" Do you want it so badly that you make it a priority, or do you just dream about it as if it is a figment of your imagination? Do you work on being successful, or do you just sit back and wish it would magically happen one day with no real effort on your part? What are you doing right now to become the success you were destined to be? If no one else says it, I am proud of you for taking the first step, and that is simply making the decision to be successful.

UNSTUCK. UNLEASHED. UNSTOPPABLE.

Do Your Actions Support Your Words?

Talk is cheap; it takes money to buy land.
– George Siggers

There are people who say they love God and that they have a true relationship with God, but their lifestyle doesn't necessarily reflect their words. My mother and I were talking one night about someone we knew who was diagnosed with Alzheimer's. The person had been a minister for years and was married, but was no longer living with his wife. Because he and his wife were both sick, their children had split them up to take care of them individually. The man's daughter would say that she questioned whether he had Alzheimer's because he would remember to pray and fast on Tuesdays, which had been a practice at the church where he ministered for many years. He would also say he wanted to see his wife. As a child, I can recall how he would always talk about how he loved his wife. Even with Alzheimer's, his actions backed up what he said. The same story goes for another lady I knew who died with Alzheimer's years prior; she would remember who her pastor was even when she didn't remember her own children and would still pray. I think that is pretty indicative of a strong relationship with God that is not based on talk alone.

You can't hide from yourself.

Your words and actions must align and intersect at some point.

A couple of the things I like to say are that "I am stronger and getting better," or that "Things are spectacular and getting better." It sounds good to say, but reality is, what am I doing to become stronger? How am I working to become better? If I am not doing anything to move forward, then I am lying to myself and you can never run away from yourself. You can't hide from yourself. You will always be with you. You can fool others, but only you truly know if you are lying to yourself. When you begin to believe the lies you tell yourself, you have hit rock bottom.

Back up your words. Own what you say. Deliver on your promises. You can tell me anything, but at some point, you have to put your money where your mouth is. Your words and actions must align and intersect at some point. Otherwise, you're just like most people—a talker. If you want to stand out, to be different, then do what you say you are going to do. Walk with the doers of life. If I have to choose a talker or a doer, I will choose the doer every time. Stop talking, and in the words of Nike, "Just do it." All I am looking to do is to back up what I say. You have way too much to accomplish to get caught up with empty words. Break down your goals into simple and easy actionable steps. Allow your actions to show what you want your words to say.

Who do you need to move to another area of your life because they only talk and leave you with wishful thinking? What have you said you were going to do but just haven't done yet?

UNSTUCK. UNLEASHED. UNSTOPPABLE.

What Goal Are You Ready to Give Up On, but the Reason Why You Want to Accomplish It Makes You Hold On Just a Little While Longer?

Before you give up, think of the reason why you hung on so long.
– Drake

> He could have given up and let the cancer beat him, but he hung on for so long because the kids needed him.

Desmond Merriweather, Dez, as he was affectionately called, was known as the "King of Binghampton." Fighting for his life, with only twenty-four hours to live, he made a request to have someone call Anfernee "Penny" Hardaway to coach his basketball team. Dez would survive for a few more years. Looking death in the face and in between doctor's appointments, surgeries, radiation, and chemotherapy, Dez would continue to coach "his kids." He could have given up and let the cancer beat him, but he hung on for so long because the kids needed him. In that neighborhood, the kids could easily get into gangs, drugs, and criminal activities. Most of those kids didn't have a dad or a role model. Dez was their dad, mentor, coach, and role model. One week before his transition into eternity, he was on television saying that he was hanging on and looking forward to his boys winning a championship. When asked why he was holding on, he said they were giving him so much. During the interview, the reporter told Dez that by his continuing to be involved, it was taking so much out of him. Dez said that his being involved was putting so much in him. I am sure if he didn't focus on his will to live for his boys and the Binghampton community, he probably would have passed much earlier.

In Dez's words, "God showed me my purpose early." Desmond was willing to die for what he believed in, and that was making a difference in the lives of the boys of "Beautiful Black Binghampton." The "kids" kept Dez alive for six years after his initial diagnosis of cancer with only a few weeks to live. Dez kept fighting even when he could have given up because he wanted to see his boys win a championship and excel academically by going on to college.

Why have you hung on to the dream this long? Are you absolutely sure that it is time to give up or are you just tired and you need to call a "time out" instead? Achieve your goals for yourself and "Do It For Dez," as we like to say.

UNSTUCK. UNLEASHED. UNSTOPPABLE.

Are You Living Life on Your Own Terms?

*Your life is precious. You've only got one.
Don't waste it on bad relationships, on bad marriages,
on bad people. Waste it wisely on what you want to do.
– Eric Idle*

You have been given one life to live. You may as well enjoy it. There's no win living miserably until your number is called. That would be a tragedy. So many of us stay in situations where there is no joy or peace because either we are afraid of disappointing someone else or because we think that this is the way it's supposed to be. We try to convince ourselves that it is unrealistic to think that we can be truly happy and that fairy tales don't come true. While we may not be happy every day, if we changed our situations, we could have joy and peace.

> We can choose to make the best out of bad situations.

We can't control anything or anyone else. We can choose to make the best out of bad situations. We can choose to be grateful and to always look at the positives. We can choose to do all we can to enjoy life and find a little piece of happiness. Why do we stay when we should leave? Why do we settle when we can have more? Why do we give up on our dreams and our goals, sacrificing ourselves because we think we don't deserve a better life? Why do we allow someone else to control us? Why do we allow others the benefit of maximizing their potential at our expense? We wake up one day, finally getting it ...finally realizing that we've wasted time. We realize that we had options. We realize

> *Time is my most precious commodity, and I protect it as if it were my baby.*

that we had power, we just gave it to someone else. We sacrificed our dreams at the expense of our souls.

I am very introspective. I often find myself thinking about my life and what I want to have achieved when my time is up. One thing I know for sure is that I do not have any time to waste. I've had so many that I loved leave too soon. Time is my most precious commodity, and I protect it as if it were my baby. I have dreams to accomplish and goals to achieve, and there are only so many hours in the day. For me, time is not to be wasted on things that add no value to my life. Bad relationships or a bad marriage—either work on making it better and give it all you've got or exit the relationship. If it is a bad marriage, seek wise counsel. I once had a co-worker that I liked very much, but she was so negative. All she wanted to do was to discuss the negative things that would occur. She would become upset with me because I refused to get sucked into the negative abyss. I had to make a decision to let her go. She was toxic to my happiness. Her energy was bad. I couldn't afford to let her negativity drain me. I had to let her go. I had no choice in the matter. I refuse to be in a bad situation voluntarily. Last time I checked, they were not handing out second lives on the deathbed because you suddenly realized what was important. What I am saying is…do not waste valuable resources on intolerable circumstances. Figure out what your purpose is in this life and maximize your potential.

What are you wasting time and energy on that is robbing you of your joy? What areas of your life do you need to improve? If you were to die today, have you lived a life worth living? Are you living the life of your dreams or are you sacrificing you for someone else? If so, do they appreciate it and is it worth it?

UNSTUCK. UNLEASHED. UNSTOPPABLE.

When Was the Last Time You Thanked Your Haters?

Haters will see you walk on water and say it's because you can't swim.
– Unknown

> *Some of us really can lose everything, rebuild, and come back from a loss stronger and better.*

I remember having to overcome a temporary setback. Unfortunate circumstances required me to temporarily move back home to Memphis from Maryland. When I moved back home, I didn't have a job right away. It took me a couple of months to find stable employment. I had money saved. I was able to move into an apartment, but I didn't want to spend money on furniture and entertainment because I didn't know how long I would be out of work. In my apartment, I had a bedroom suite but no sofa or chairs. I was on the grind. I didn't need a sofa or television because I needed to make some things happen and quickly. Not having a television and a sofa was a little uncomfortable, but I didn't need comfort. I needed to hustle and get back in the game. I was able to secure a teaching position and activate my real estate license. I eventually purchased another home in Memphis.

While teaching, I met a lady and we became pretty cool. While building a friendship, I shared snippets of my story. Our friendship eventually progressed where we would visit each other's home. One day she made a comment that my boyfriend must have bought my house and furniture. I was taken aback. I hustled, saved, sacrificed, and purchased everything myself. I didn't have a home full of furniture for a long time because I wanted to pay cash for what I wanted, while continuing to save money and enjoy life's other pleasantries. The funny thing was that someone I had known for years and who had been to my other homes made the same comment. She knew me "pre-boyfriend." She knew that I would work for what I wanted and go after what I wanted with tenacity. So, while the first person hadn't known me that long, the other person had. She knew what I was about and had seen me accomplish so many goals. I guess it was just easier for her to believe that I wasn't that powerful and strong. It was easier for her to try and take away my accomplishments because she didn't want to believe that I could start over so many times like I had before and still rise like the sun. Some of us really can lose everything, rebuild, and come back from a loss stronger and better. If I did it once, I can do it again, because you can never take away the knowledge. Pay haters no attention because they only serve two purposes: 1) They validate your success by letting you know that you are worth watching, and 2) They provide you the energy you need to propel you to accomplish major success. You owe your haters a "thank you."

What have you accomplished lately to ensure your haters know your name? What have you done so well that even your haters have to say you are the best? Are you keeping your haters frustrated because they just can't keep up with you, they just can't stop talking about you, and they dare not stop watching you?

UNSTUCK. UNLEASHED. UNSTOPPABLE.

How Do You Best Solve Problems? How Has That Been Working for You?

Letting your mind play is the best way to solve problems.
– Bill Watterson

Some people have a special talent for solving problems. One of the talents I have been blessed with is the ability to solve problems. Thinking outside of the box and creatively is something that comes relatively easy for me. I have been able to develop the ability to solve problems by not rushing, if possible, to make a decision. I like to toy around with the problem for a bit and allow my mind to explore several possible solutions. As I allow my mind to think and roam freely, I allow possible solutions to marinate, all while thinking of the true problem at hand.

> *As I allow my mind to think and roam freely, I allow possible solutions to marinate, all while thinking of the true problem at hand.*

Before you know it, there's not only a solution, but also possible alternatives that could work. Turn off the television, the negative voices in your head, and the radio, if necessary. Just relax and allow your mind to roam freely while thinking of possible solutions. As a solution comes, no matter how crazy it may seem, write it down. Walk away and come back to it later.

I can recall having to make a decision as to the best way to present a major problem to my manager. I just couldn't figure out the best way to present the issue to her without alienating her. I was less-than-happy with the hires who were her favorites and who had a dotted-line-reporting structure to me. The individuals were the most challenging people I had ever worked with, and there were dynamics there that needed attention. I won't go into the particulars, but there were several issues that needed to be addressed, and how I addressed and solved the problem would make all the difference. I remember walking in the door one day and getting ready for bed hours earlier than normal. I reclined on the sofa and consciously made a decision to allow my mind to roam free, which is not the usual for me. As time passed by (hours actually), I felt myself relaxing, and the ideas of how to present the problem to her and how to manage this group eventually came to me. The ideas weren't necessarily comfortable for me and were definitely outside of the way I would have normally handled the situation at hand. Because this was a sensitive situation and the stakes were high, I needed to proceed with caution. A lot was riding on how well I handled the situation. An out-of-the-box solution was warranted and thankfully, that's what I got by allowing my mind to wander freely.

What problems are you finding challenging to find a solution for? Have you allowed yourself the opportunity to take a break, step away, come back to it later, and allow your mind to explore all possible solutions, no matter how silly or uncomfortable they may be? What risk do you face by rushing to a decision before you have considered all available options?

UNSTUCK. UNLEASHED. UNSTOPPABLE.

How Do You Make the Best Use of Your Time?

No one can stop a ticking clock, but the great ones always find a way to slow it down.
– Quote from the movie Draft Day

Have you ever felt like you were racing against time? Have you ever felt the pressure to make a decision before you had really settled on the direction you would take? What do you do? When your back is against the wall, you've got to find a way to slow down the clock. The best way to slow down the clock is by thinking creatively and strategically.

By employing the expertise of others, you will find that as you look to others to serve as experts, oftentimes they are more drawn to you.

Give others the opportunity to play a part in your success.

If you have leverage, you can use the skills, strengths, talents, and time of others to your advantage. The great thing about this strategy is that you are allowing others to excel in the areas in which they are gifted. By employing the expertise of others, you will find that as you look to others to serve as experts, oftentimes they are more drawn to you. People like to provide direction and advice to others. Give others the opportunity to play a part in your success.

In the movie *Draft Day*, the main character has to make a decision that can alter the future success of his NFL team. He finds himself racing against time and has to figure out a strategy to put more time on the clock. He calls up other teams and trades places with them to pick players for the draft. This allows him to buy more time and explore his options. By the time he's ready, he is ready to execute on his original pick. Sometimes, it may cost us a little bit to buy more time, but it is often worth the price or the sacrifice. When we truly understand what our time is worth, we will often pay for convenience. The convenience or the shortened learning curve may be just what we need to help us live more joyfully and abundantly. Once the clock starts, it can't be stopped. It's running and you have to make a decision. To slow down the clock requires strategy. Sometimes, it may require you figuring out what the next person needs so you can get what you want. This happens all the time in successful negotiations.

Slowing down the clock may require skill, partnership, and/or negotiation. How can you buy yourself more time by slowing down the clock so you can focus on what's important in life? How can you stop trading time for money?

UNSTUCK. UNLEASHED. UNSTOPPABLE.

How Are You Really Doing?

Don't lose hope. When the sun goes down, the stars come out.
– Unknown

The sun is beautiful and produces needed light, but the stars are simply breathtaking. The beauty is the stars are there all along. In the daylight, they're just hidden from view. Sometimes, a situation can appear hopeless, but it is important that we never lose hope, because it won't always be like this. The sun always comes after the rain and the stars always come out at night. Stay focused on the positive. Keep believing. If you are still breathing, that means there is a possibility that things can change and become better than you ever expected. You can be one positive thought, word, or decision away from your life changing. If you have no more hope left, borrow mine. I believe you are on the brink of greatness. Go outside tonight and look at the stars, and let the stars be a reminder that you are closer than you think.

> Sometimes, a situation can appear hopeless, but it is important that we never lose hope, because it won't always be like this.

> If you are still breathing, that means there is a possibility that things can change and become better than you ever expected.

I remember when I was in the fight for my life. It appeared that the sun was never going to shine again. Things were dismal for a while. Things were so dark that to me, my future looked bleak. However, there was something inside of me that knew that things were going to get better—they had to get better. So many people have destroyed their lives because they have lost hope. Some people turn to other people to get them out of the dark abyss. Others look to drugs or alcohol, and some even are so hopeless that they decide to take their own life. No matter how dark and hopeless your situation may seem, it can't last forever. Summer always comes after spring, and spring comes after winter. Just as the seasons change, so will things change in your life if you hang on and don't give up.

What dreams have you given up on? What do you need to renew hope in? Have you taken inventory of your life and counted your blessings? What do you need to be grateful for? Remember, things could be better, but they could be worse. It may be helpful to keep a gratitude journal.

UNSTUCK. UNLEASHED. UNSTOPPABLE.

Are You the Active Architect of Your Life?

I'm spectacular and getting better.
– Sharalyn Payne

How often do you hear people ask, "How are you?" Many people ask and never really listen to hear your response, because they ask the question out of courtesy or habit. A lot of us go through the motions and we say, "I'm fine," whenever we are asked that question. What if you used that one question to make a difference in someone else's life? What if we really stopped and waited for a response? What if we used our response to that question to speak positively over our own life? What if, when someone asked us how we were doing, we said something like, "Spectacular and getting better" or "Stronger and wiser," changing up our responses so they weren't routine, but powerful responses used to shape our lives. What if, instead of us saying, "And you?" we said, "Is there anything I can do for you?" What if we began to create community by building relationships and showing people that we cared about them? Would we have more influence and impact?

> What if, when someone asked us how we were doing, we said something like, "Spectacular and getter better," or "Stronger and wiser," changing up our responses so they weren't routine, but powerful responses used to shape our lives.

Since we are using our words to help us create the life we want, can we expect to attract positive things now that we are more aware of the power of our words? As we began to speak differently, how long would it take for our actions to line up with our words? Would we begin to act differently, maybe even more intentionally, with how we "do life?" You see, if you begin to speak differently, you will begin to think and act differently. It all starts with you taking that first step. As the changes become more apparent, you'll begin to wonder why you hadn't done this sooner. It may be a culture shock to you initially, but after continued practice, it will become a little challenging to go back to that old way of living.

Identify your power language, whatever works for you, and make it a point to use active words in your life.

Spectacular and getting better…or stronger and wiser…these are not magic words that will bring instant miracles, but they are positive words that can help you to feel empowered. If you're not spectacular and getting better, do you want to be? If you're not stronger and wiser, why wouldn't you want to be? Identify your power language, whatever works for you, and make it a point to use active words in your life. You've got to make things happen, and you can't do that if you're passive. Get in the game.

How are you going through the motions in life? How can you become the master architect over your life? How do you use your words to shape your life?

UNSTUCK. UNLEASHED. UNSTOPPABLE.

Can You See Your Dreams Even When You're Sleeping?

*Dreams are not what you see in sleep.
It's the thing which doesn't let you sleep.
– A. P. J. Abdul Kalam*

What are your dreams? Are your dreams so vivid that they haunt you by day or night? Do they keep creeping into your thoughts when you should be thinking of something else? Do you find yourself daydreaming about what life would be like if your dream became a reality? When you should be focused on other things such as family celebrations, is your mind somewhere else? Do you try to turn it off, but you can't? Does it seem like ideas are constantly being downloaded that line up with your vision?

If you want your dream badly enough, you'll see it everywhere— even in your sleep.

What is your heart's biggest desire? What would happen if you were able to achieve your dreams? How would you feel if you were ushered into a room with all of your dreams fulfilled, but you couldn't access it because you never even tried?

I hope your dreams visit you in your sleep and you see them there in color.

What if you put forth the effort in achieving the one dream that you would rather have more than anything? What is it? What's pulling at your heart?

My dreams don't let me sleep. It seems as if I am haunted by them. Even when I'm asleep, my dreams are there. My sleep is consumed with ideas that further support my goals. It's as if my dreams are chasing me, speaking and willing themselves into existence. If you want your dream badly enough, you'll see it everywhere—even in your sleep.

It's not too late for you to begin chasing your dreams. As a matter of fact, it is never too late. I want you to be so determined to achieve your dreams that your dreams start chasing you. I hope your dreams visit you in your sleep and you see them there in color. I want you to see your dreams in such vivid detail that they must become a reality, because they have no choice.

 What dead dreams do you need to awaken and make happen? What is the recurring dream of your life?

UNSTUCK. UNLEASHED. UNSTOPPABLE.

Are You More Like the Scarecrow or the Lion?

The doors will be opened to those who are bold enough to knock.
– Tony Gaskin

You have to knock on the door of opportunity. You have to go out and look for opportunity, and then ask for it. Rarely will opportunity just land in your lap. Opportunity is looking for you, but are you looking for it? Sometimes, you have to knock more than once. It may require persistence on your part before the door is opened.

> *You have to go out and look for opportunity and then ask for it.*

The most financially secure person I know is so because he went looking for opportunity. After relocating to a place where he didn't know anyone, he asked around about a church that he should visit. The same church and pastor continued to come up again and again. He attempted to secure a meeting with the pastor of this predominantly large congregation. He tried for months and months to meet with the pastor and just couldn't secure that appointment. He kept trying. Finally, he was able to get a meeting with the premise that they would meet only for a few minutes. The two hit it off. The result was the pastor became a huge influence on the eventual multi-millionaire's life.

> *Be courageous enough to knock on the door and bold enough to kick it open if necessary.*

The pastor took the young man under his wing, opened some doors, made some connections, and the rest is history. Both his spiritual and financial future was impacted because of that connection. What if he hadn't have been bold enough to knock on the door? What If he had knocked once, but not persisted and insisted on that meeting? One person, one idea, one word can change your life forever.

Keep knocking and knock some more. Remember, the door finally opened and that one meeting was life-changing for both men. The pastor credited the young man with getting him out of his comfort zone and said he was like a son to him. The young man became not only a business partner for the pastor, a family friend, a son, and an advisor to many of the pastor's community, but also a trusted confidante. If you knock boldly, the door will finally open for you and your life could change for the better forever. Be courageous enough to knock on the door and bold enough to kick it open if necessary.

What doors do you need to knock on to achieve your goals? How bold are you? Are you bold enough to ask for what you want? Are you strong enough to keep asking until you get it?

UNSTUCK. UNLEASHED. UNSTOPPABLE.

Do You Know Who You Are and Whose You Are?

The secret is to have a sense of yourself, your real self, your unique self. And not just once in a while, or once a day, but all through the day, the week and life.
– Bill Murray

If you don't know who you are, then you will be more open to the opinions of others, allowing them to define you. Their definition of you may not always be accurate. If you take in what people say, then you can drive yourself crazy. It is important to know who you are and that will require you spending time with yourself. You are not defined by what you have accomplished or material possessions. You are defined by your purpose, your character, your values, your thoughts, your ambitions, your DNA, your past, your present, your dreams, your future, your actions, and your reactions. People may have an idea of who you are because of what you allow them to see. Just because they have known you for quite some time doesn't mean that they know everything there is to know about you. We grow. We change, and we may even suppress our true thoughts and dreams for fear of failure (and sometimes because we fear success). Some of us haven't spent enough time by ourselves, soul-searching our purpose, so that we may fulfill our life's work. We haven't taken the time to ask ourselves, "What is it that I want for my life?" We live the life that someone else has told us that they think we should pursue, only to find that life fails to give us life. We die slowly while living. We give our power away because we don't have the courage to study our hearts and to uncover our purpose so that we may remain true to who we are at our core.

> *With everything people will say about me, it's nothing compared to what I say, believe, and know about myself.*

Never stop learning about you.

If I allowed others to define me, I could only imagine what they would say. Some people would exaggerate and others would downplay who I am. With everything people will say about me, it's nothing compared to what I say, believe, and know about myself. It's up to me and you to discover the hidden gems that we are. As we continue to uncover what's been buried and hidden, there is still more we may not know until it's time for us to learn that particular part of ourselves. So, it's important that we regularly check in to see what's being deposited into our hearts and downloaded into our spirit. Never stop learning about you.

Who are you? How does that differ from other's perception of you?

Your Heart Is Deceptive

Never make a decision based on emotions, because your emotions will change.
– Ella Payne

I cannot tell you how many times I have to reflect on this. Emotions can be deceptive and will change. So, it is important to make decisions based upon facts and data. If I made a decision every time my emotions changed, I would be unstable. I remember having a friend who made me so angry that I wanted to truly end the friendship at that time. I was furious. Instead of making the decision to end the friendship, I made the decision to calm down, step back, and re-evaluate what actually occurred. I had to determine if the one issue was worth us losing a solid friendship over or if the relationship was truly worth repairing. I decided to not base my decision upon emotion, but upon facts. The fact was that we had years of a solid friendship and that the act wasn't so grievous that the relationship was irreparable. I can tell you that because we both can be stubborn, I'm not so sure that we would have been able to repair the relationship down the road if I would have ended it based upon what I felt at that time. What's crazy is that I can't recall why I was so upset!

I've had a friend who stayed in what she described to be an unhealthy marriage for years. One day, she decided that she was going to leave her husband. Once she saw how hard the single life was, she began to regret her decision, but it was too late because her husband had moved on. Prior to her leaving, she and I had many conversations about how she felt. When she would ask me my opinion, I would tell her that "I didn't have a dog in the fight," and my only advice was that she seek professional counseling and not make a decision based upon her emotions because they could change. I recommended that she wait to make a decision until she knew with certainty that she wouldn't later regret her decision. When she left, she said she felt positive she was making the right decision. My heart went out to her when she shared the pain in her heart because she regretted the decision and wanted her family back. Her husband refused to entertain the idea of reconciliation.

When have you made a decision based upon your emotions? Did your emotions change? How comfortable were you about your decision after you allowed your emotions to subside?

UNSTUCK. UNLEASHED. UNSTOPPABLE.

How Often Do We Question That What We See and Hear Is Accurately Being Depicted?

Believe none of what you hear and half of what you see.
– Abraham Lincoln

Do you make it a practice to seek truth and facts and then take action, if necessary? Things are not always what we think. We have a brain and mind to seek clarity before we think negatively of others, or worse, participate in the gossip or destruction of another person's character and reputation. People will tell us what they think they saw or what they heard. It's up to us to pursue truth at all times and not always take what is being presented to us as factual. The media (including the news studios) do a good job of telling us the story they want us to know. They get paid to present a certain image, which causes us to live our lives a certain way.

> *We have a brain and mind to seek clarity before we think negatively of others or worse, participate in the gossip or destruction of another person's character and reputation.*

One of the things I have always found interesting is that you can say something to someone, and they hear something totally different from what you said. It's as if you were speaking a foreign language, and the interpreter lost it in the translation to the other person. People will take what you say and hear what they want to hear. The impact is that feelings can be hurt and relationships can be damaged. When the stakes are high, it probably is a good idea to ensure the timing is optimal and all parties are focused on the conversation at hand. After stating the topic of discussion, it may be helpful to ask the other parties to paraphrase what they heard and share their insight regarding the topic. This can help to ensure everyone has clarity and is properly aligned. You don't have to wonder about what the person meant. I have an acquaintance who often laughs whenever he asks me my thoughts on a topic that we have discussed. He likes to say I am like a human tape recorder because I can often recite back to him word for word what he has said, in the order in which he said it. I've had to develop this skill throughout my career so I can provide the best value to the client and/or the organization. Actively listening is very important. This skill can be developed by "being present." Do your best to refrain from daydreaming, multitasking, or focusing on your next discussion point when talking with people. Ask questions to ensure you are on the same page.

> *It's up to us to pursue truth at all times and not always take what is being presented to us as factual.*

"Never believe your lying eyes," is a statement my mother would always tell me when I was a little girl. So you see an older man in his eighties, walking across the street arm-in-arm with a beautiful, well-dressed young lady who appears to be in her late twenties. They enter a high-end restaurant, and she is throwing her hair back and laughing at his jokes as she is leaning in towards him. When they get ready to leave the restaurant, she straightens his tie and kisses him on the cheek before exiting. She tells him how much she loves him and he gives her his credit card. What are you thinking? Most people would think she is a gold digger and is taking advantage of her lover, which is an older man, but I hope you are thinking that she must really love her grandfather. So many people will look at this scene and think that this young lady should be ashamed of herself for taking advantage of this older man, that she couldn't possibly love him, and go on and on about what they haven't the slightest clue about. People will see something and will make up stories based upon what they think they see and hear, which couldn't be further from the truth. Good questions to ask yourself are: "Why is this information being presented to me? What action does the sharer of this news want me to take?" Remember, above all, pursue truth.

When have you neglected to obtain facts and acted on perception? What was the end result?

UNSTUCK. UNLEASHED. UNSTOPPABLE.

What Are You Willing to Sacrifice for Your Dreams?

If you want something you've never had, you must be willing to do something you've never done.
– Thomas Jefferson

> I believe an enemy of success, fulfillment, and joy is the inability to shift when needed.

Success requires action and oftentimes sacrifice. I believe an enemy of success, fulfillment, and joy is the inability to shift when needed. Everything will not easily come to us and be just as we would have planned. The ability to operate outside of our comfort zone is a skill and a strength which is not to be taken for granted. Greatness requires grit and grind, even if only for a season.

I can recall wanting to escape from mediocrity. I knew that the life I was living was great for some, but yet something inside of me felt there was more. I couldn't escape the feeling that was deep within my soul that knew that an ordinary life was not what was meant for me. My inner being knew that I was supposed to live extraordinarily and that was my heart's desire—my unspoken prayer. The continued tugging and pulling of my inner core prompted me to begin a search to identify my purpose. It was as if I couldn't escape the desire to live differently. Once I identified my purpose, I began to operate in it, and it was as if life looked differently to me. My problems didn't go away, but I was better able to understand why certain things were happening. I felt empowered. The best way to describe it is that for the first time, I felt free. It was like heavy chains and dead weight were dropping off of me. I felt lighter, as if the journey of life was bearable.

UNSTUCK. UNLEASHED. UNSTOPPABLE.

As I began to take control of my life and operate with passion, I found myself making better decisions. I began to pay more attention to the environment around me, noticing the signs that were directing me along the journey. How I processed the information now that I was operating out of purpose would be in direct correlation to me living out my life by design and not by chance. I realized that I had a part to play in my success that required me to actively contribute—to be proactive rather than reactive. The still, small voice that I ignored sometimes was not to be ignored any longer. My new life—the life I wanted, craved, and had dreamed of—could no longer accept and support business as usual. My gut, intuition, wisdom, and discernment would guide me as I processed information and made choices.

The ability to operate outside of our comfort zone is a skill and a strength which is not to be taken for granted.

Since I have made the decision to be more conscious and thoughtful of the world around me, I am happier. Things are working out better. I trust myself more and trust what God has placed inside of me. Now I can say that as the universe is working to support my purpose, I have tapped into my personal power. I am maximizing my potential and creating a life that I am absolutely in love with, and I want that for you too.

What do you need to do that you have not yet done to get what you have never had?

UNSTUCK. UNLEASHED. UNSTOPPABLE.

When You Finish Speaking, What Do People Think of You?

*Better to remain silent and be thought a fool,
than to speak out and remove all doubt.
– Abraham Lincoln*

Knowing how to say something and when to say something is a skill that can take you before great men and women.

I remember meeting a man and it took him a couple of weeks to actually connect with me. When he finally did, he insulted and offended me continuously throughout the conversation. I am not a person who is easily offended. I know you may be wondering why I didn't just end the conversation, but I do believe that there is a reason why we exchange energy with a person. I strive to practice not walking away so fast or throwing people away because they are different from me. How do you learn, how do you grow, how do you get what God has for you if you isolate yourself from people who offend you or are different from you?

You can learn from a fool. You may have heard that silence is golden. Sometimes, it is best to remain silent. When you are quiet, you can learn a lot, if you are paying attention. Besides, people do not always need to know your angle or where you are coming from. When you speak, you are providing them with your point of view, but do you know theirs? Do you know your audience and what is important to them? If you don't, you can open your mouth and unleash fury and opposition that you weren't prepared for, especially if you don't have all of the facts and details. Knowing what to say is important, but knowing how to say something (exercising tact) is a lost, but valuable art. Knowing how to say something and when to say something is a skill that can take you before great men and women.

> *Our words should be used to build, encourage, educate, inspire, uplift, empower, and motivate, and never to tear down, humiliate, poison, taint, or discourage anyone.*

Back to the gentleman who insulted me. Not only did he insult me, but he also insulted the president, and all women throughout the conversation. When he found out what my profession was, as well as my gifts, talents, and connections, he thought it would be a good idea for us to collaborate on future projects. He wanted access to my network. By then, he had proved that he was a fool, and I had no desire to connect with him on a personal or professional level. How would I know what he would say if I put him in front of the wrong people? I could damage my reputation and credibility. I value my connections and relationships and would not knowingly expose them to a fool or a person with foolish behavior. It was interesting to see that although he was attractive, well-spoken, and poised, he was unintelligent and needed refining.

As I have grown myself and I am continuing to grow, I am cognizant of not only the image I portray visually, but the choice of words I use when communicating to others. While I may not always speak with the elegance and grace of the former first lady, Michelle Obama, I am aware that I should only speak on topics of which I am knowledgeable. Our words should be used to build, encourage, educate, inspire, uplift, empower, and motivate, and never to tear down, humiliate, poison, taint, or discourage anyone. You have the power to change things with the words that you speak. Choose your words carefully and learn when to speak. Remember, there are two sides in every person. In a man, there is a king and there is a fool. It is important to know which person you are talking to. If you talk to the fool, you may not like the results.

 Have you ever met someone that you thought was a fool? Did this person change, grow, and become wise? Do you need to practice thinking more before you speak? Do you make it a habit to only speak on things which you are knowledgeable of?

How Do You Appreciate in Value Because Others Are Appreciative of What You Mean to Them?

*Investments appreciate. Homes appreciate.
In healthy relationships, people should appreciate as well.*
– Antonio Adair

How do you feel when you hear the words, "I appreciate that," or "I appreciate you?" Maybe you feel a little better when you hear those words. Maybe you hear those words and they fall on deaf ears. What if the person telling you those words really did appreciate you, and their actions reflected the true essence of the word *appreciate*? If we truly appreciate people, then wouldn't we interact with them differently? If I appreciated you and my worth increased because of you, then how could I treat you as if you are common instead of invaluable?

Sometimes, we become too familiar with people. We take them for granted and interact with them as if they have not increased us in knowledge, power, and love. Our gratitude for their sacrifices, thoughtfulness, assistance, insight, and wisdom has made a contribution to the betterment and enhancement of our lives. As we appreciate in value, so should they. We should show honor, reverence, and respect to them because they didn't have to do anything for us at all. Out of their kindness and generosity, they chose to enhance our lives. We should do our part to make a contribution to their lives. If I appreciate you, then just as my value goes up because of you, so should your value go up with me. I cherish the time we spend together, ensuring I am focused, fully present, and searching for an opportunity to show you just what you mean to me. Every time I can add to your life, it will be my honor and privilege to show you that when I say "I appreciate you," those are not empty words but a heartfelt love note from me to you.

My mother has made so many sacrifices for me and I love her dearly. She is my very best friend and I appreciate all she has done. I know that what she has imparted in me has resulted in my value increasing. I wouldn't be who I am without her knowledge, prayers, and advice. Because I appreciate her so much, I look for opportunities to surprise her and to show her that she means the world to me. Some of the things I've done have made her laugh, and others have touched her heart in such a way that it made her cry. Very rarely will I allow her to do anything for me. I have to remind myself that I have to allow her to be a blessing to me by sowing good seeds so she can reap a harvest later. I can never repay her for what she has done, but I can show her as often as I can that I will never forget what she has done for me.

Not too long ago, I was helping a friend who was going through a divorce. I would drive across town to her home to help her for hours at a time. While there, she always made sure I was comfortable. She would insist on showing me her appreciation by paying for dinner or going to the movies afterward. She didn't have to and I certainly didn't expect her to do so. I was just there to help and show my support. My services weren't for sale because that's what friends do. A couple of days later, she would always call to let me know she really appreciated me and I could feel her sincere appreciation.

A habit I make is to not just tell people I appreciate them, but to really help them to understand what their efforts have meant to me and how it has impacted my life. Whether it's a card, a bonus, an award, flowers, a dinner, or another token of appreciation, I strive to really think about the person and give them something that is of value to them.

UNSTUCK. UNLEASHED. UNSTOPPABLE.

 Who do you appreciate and why? How do you show them you appreciate them? How can you "give honor to whom honor is due?" Who makes you better? Who says they appreciate you but have a hard time showing you?

UNSTUCK. UNLEASHED. UNSTOPPABLE.

Have You Ever Received What You Prayed for to Later Regret it?

Be careful what you pray for because you just might get it.
– Unknown

Boy, oh boy, have I learned my lesson on what to ask for and pray for. There are some prayer requests that came true, and I felt like I could have slit my wrists. God knew that was not the best for me, so why did He give it to me? Just because I kept asking for it. Didn't He know that could have killed me? I mean how was I supposed to know that what I thought was good for me was detrimental to my well-being. I don't know everything. Now, I know to be very careful what I ask God for. That's certainly a lesson that I won't have to learn twice. Okay, so now my prayers go a little something like this: "Lord, change my will to Your will. Help me not to desire anything that is not your very best for me. Help me to trust you and to rest in your infinite wisdom and plan for my life. Thank you that I seek you first and I willingly yield to your desires and plans for my life. I praise you in advance for shielding and protecting me from myself and my foolish desires. Thank you for wanting better and more for me than I want for myself and not allowing me to settle. Thank you for granting me my heart's desires that are aligned with your will for my life. Amen."

Prayers change real quick when you have to walk and go through some things that look like they will take you out. The man or woman you thought you had to have that wreaked havoc in your life helped you to understand that you need to be sure of what you want and what you ask for. Sometimes, we may not be equipped to handle what comes along with what we desire. The house you had to have that drains all of your finances and doesn't allow you to do anything else. The car you thought you had to have, but is always in need of expensive repairs. The career that you wanted that offers no work-life balance. If only we could see into the future…but we can't. If only we could turn back the hands of time…but we can't. All we can do is to be careful of what we pray for from this point forward.

 Have you ever gotten something that you yearned for to only find that it was not what you truly desired? What did you do? What lesson did you learn?

UNSTUCK. UNLEASHED. UNSTOPPABLE.

You Can Run, But You Cannot Hide

You can't run from you.
– Sharalyn Payne

Have you ever met someone who was always running from something or someone? You can't run from you. No matter who you are and what you do, as long as you live, you will always be with yourself. So, you may as well own who you are and deal with all of you. You have got to deal with your past, your bad decisions, the consequences of your choices, your insecurities, your fears, your struggles, your thoughts, your actions, and your reactions.

My future happiness and success would be based upon my attitude.

You will always be there. You are the constant in the equation. When I relocated from Upper Marlboro, Austin, Dallas, and Memphis, my thoughts and beliefs relocated right along with me. I was broken, sad, hurt, strong, brave, courageous, adventurous, and hopeful among many other emotions. There came a time when I had to get real with myself and own the fact that I played an intricate part in my happiness. No one else was responsible for my life. No matter where I went, I was there.

I had the power to destroy the things that were trying to sabotage my future success.

My future happiness and success would be based upon my attitude. No one was going to come and save me. No one could turn things around. No one could make me happy. The decision to be joyful was mine and mine alone. I had to roll up my sleeves and look back over my life and take responsibility for what I did with the defining moments. I had to pivot and problem solve when things were less than ideal. I had to be the surgeon and carve out my pain. I had to be the artist and make pain a pathway to prosperity and wealth. I had to recreate and reinvent and learn that I could not be a victim and a victor at the same time. I had to choose. While I couldn't turn back the hands of time, I could make the past work to my advantage. I had the power to make my life better, if I would be willing to conquer rejection, negativity, pessimism, fear, and doubt. I had the power to destroy the things that were trying to sabotage my future success.

When I connected my purpose with my experiences, the result was an emotional connection to my future that propelled me forward. However, I wasn't a seeker of my purpose until I first realized that I had to engage in personal development, seek a professional counselor, and pursue spiritual growth as if my life depended on it. It was the only way I could pull myself up out of the hole of despair I had dug due to my own personal choices. Once I killed the giants I had constructed, a whole new world opened up for me. I know your life will change for the better if you decide today to face the cold hard truth.

 Who and what are you trying to run from? Why? What do you think could happen if you stopped running and faced your giants?

UNSTUCK. UNLEASHED. UNSTOPPABLE.

Tools and Resources for Extraordinary Success

Visit SharalynPayne.com to:

- Join Push Partner University.

- Inquire about booking Dr. Sharalyn as a speaker or workshop presenter at your next event.

- Attend a Push Partner event.

- Register for upcoming webinars.

- Join the Insiders' Club to stay abreast of the latest tools, webinars, and training releases created to help you live the dream and make your life all that you want it to be.

- Receive your free resources on relationships, careers, success, motivation, and achievement.

UNSTUCK. UNLEASHED. UNSTOPPABLE.

Book Dr. Sharalyn to mobilize, inspire, and empower your group!

Dr. Sharalyn Payne is not simply a motivational or inspirational speaker. That's part of it, but it's only the tip of the iceberg.

Sharalyn is a dynamic, high-energy, empowerment speaker, gifted storyteller, and teacher who will transform you, your team, and your organization.

Sharalyn speaks on the topics of leadership, influence, success, careers, and achievement. She can deliver a keynote, half-day workshop, or full-day version of this content, depending on your needs.

Sharalyn's life-changing presentations are filled with hope, humor, and exercises that are sure to leave a lasting impression. Every training session, workshop, and speaking engagement is designed to shift paradigms, restore belief, increase passion, enhance energy, and instill confidence.

Using her engaging personality, provocative questions, sense of humor, and skilled teaching style, Sharalyn is just what the audience needs to move from vision to execution.

If you want a captivating speaker who can electrify and connect with your audience while exceeding your expectations, then book Sharalyn today.

Audiences will be challenged, equipped, encouraged, motivated, enlightened, and amazed! Go to www.sharalynpayne.com to book Dr. Sharalyn for your next event.

UNSTUCK. UNLEASHED. UNSTOPPABLE.

Marked. Success on Purpose.

You have been marked for success. If you are truly serious about living a life filled with success, it's time you discovered the reason you were created. You have purpose. God had a specific reason why He created you. You weren't created by chance, but you were crafted, molded, chiseled, and designed to do something that only you can do. When you search for your purpose, you will find it. When you find it and activate it, then you will see that this is the life you have been waiting for. You'll discover that everything you have gone through, good and bad, was leading you to your purpose. You'll find that you are in the best time of your life and that you don't have to wait to retire to be happy, for your kids to leave, to land the next contract, or to get the man or woman of your dreams. If you embrace the fact that you have been marked for success, and success is all about becoming the person who you not only want to be, but the person you were created to be, then you are successful.

Learn how you can discover your purpose and create a life, business, and career which reflects your brilliance, uniqueness, and individuality.

SIGN UP TODAY AT SHARALYNPAYNE.COM

UNSTUCK. UNLEASHED. UNSTOPPABLE.

Push Partner University

If you know there is more to life than how you have been living, I can help.

PUSH PARTNER UNIVERSITY is an online platform led by Sharalyn Payne and is designed to help people with big dreams and high ambitions (those who want more out of life) to win consistently and live extraordinarily! This is the platform for the person who knows there is more to life than how they have been living. This is for the person who knows deep within their heart that they are unstoppable, unshakeable, and unbreakable. This platform is for the person who's been saying: "I know I am destined to be great, I know life has more for me, I know that I'm not living up to my full potential. All I need is a little help. If someone would just tell me what to do and how to do it, there would be no stopping me."

By joining this exclusive online community, you'll get access to private trainings, tools, resources, and proven strategies designed to change your life. This is an exclusive community designed for the person who wants more out of life. This is the place where you can rest assured that you will receive what you need to be obtain clarity, build your confidence, overcome obstacles, make major moves, and improve your overall quality of life. Here, you will be motivated and inspired to not just create a life, but to leave a legacy—a lasting mark that shows the world that you were here and you made a difference.

pushpartneruniversity.com

Bring *Unstuck. Unleashed. Unstoppable.* to Your Home or Enterprise

If you are interested in a private VIP day of motivating, inspiring, equipping, and empowering yourself or your team, contact Push Partner, LLC, at:

Email: info@pushpartner.com
Online: www.pushpartner.com
Periscope: @SharalynPayne
Facebook: Facebook.com/SharalynPayneBiz
Podcast: Push Partner with Sharalyn Payne
Instagram: @SharalynPayne
Twitter: @SharalynPayne

Sign up for Sharalyn's free newsletter at www.sharalynpayne.com.

To purchase bulk copies of *Unstuck. Unleashed. Unstoppable.* at a discount for large groups, please contact your favorite bookseller or Push Partner at pushpartnerpublishing@pushpartner.com.

About the Author

Dr. Sharalyn Payne is a motivational speaker, an empowerment teacher, an inspiration, and a catalyst of change for countless people all over the world. In addition, Sharalyn is a coach, mentor, and friend who is obsessed with inspiring and encouraging others to live a life of freedom and extraordinary success. Her wisdom and insight pushes achievers and challenges leaders to be undeniably great. Sharalyn's personal life experiences filled with successes and failures, trials and triumphs, highs and lows, loves and losses, and her unique story-telling ability has resulted in huge paradigm shifts and true life change. Her sense of humor, belief in the impossible, captivating smile, and love for people leaves audiences with renewed hope, restored belief, and transformed lives.

You can learn more about Sharalyn by visiting her blog at www.sharalynpayne.com, a site dedicated to inspiring, equipping, motivating, encouraging, and empowering high achievers and leaders to become the hero in their movie, the creator of their destiny, the artist behind their masterpiece, and the author of their story.

Dr. Sharalyn is also the founder of Push Partner, a movement created to push you to move beyond your comfort zone, position you to embrace your power, and hold you accountable for living the life of your dreams.

www.ingramcontent.com/pod-product-compliance
Lightning Source LLC
Chambersburg PA
CBHW071605080526
44588CB00010B/1024